WELL
DOCUMENTED

First published in 2022 by
White Lion Publishing,
an imprint of The Quarto Group.
The Old Brewery, 6 Blundell Street
London, N7 9BH,
United Kingdom
T (0)20 7700 6700
www.Quarto.com

A catalogue record for this book is
available from the British Library.

ISBN 978-0-7112-6799-2
Ebook ISBN 978-0-7112-6800-5

10 9 8 7 6 5 4 3 2 1

Design by Sarah Boris

Printed in Singapore

WELL DOCUMENTED

THE ESSENTIAL DOCUMENTARIES THAT PROVE THE TRUTH IS MORE FASCINATING THAN FICTION

IAN HAYDN SMITH

WHITE LION PUBLISHING

CONTENTS

FOREWORD

I didn't come from a documentary background. My first films were narrative shorts and features, which I wrote and directed. So, as I embarked on *Senna*, my first documentary, what mattered most was finding my own style. My own voice. My intention was to tell the story from the point of view of the central character, where they narrate their own life story.

When I made *Senna*, most films included talking heads. I didn't want to use them. I also didn't want to put myself in the film. I wanted to remain invisible. I wanted to make a film entirely out of archive, as I thought I had the most amazing material to work with. I was told that many directors had tried this and it didn't really work. But I hadn't tried it. As a filmmaker, it's important to follow your gut instinct and not to be afraid of being different. I'm glad I did, because the route I took worked for me and in many ways changed the way some documentaries are now being made.

There are many directors who work in both drama and documentary. Martin Scorsese has always done this. And his former student Spike Lee. There's also Kevin Macdonald, James Marsh, and more recently, Andrea Arnold. They show there is no set route to go about making a documentary and – particularly with the democratisation of digital technology – no longer any set template to what a documentary should be.

That's exactly what the films in this book show. There are films from Iran, Mexico, the US, the UK, France and so many other countries which exist in a hinterland between fiction and drama. They span a range of genre styles and incorporate elements that reflect reality, but also attempt to grapple with the slippery nature of truth. They are not bound by constraints, but find inventive ways to illuminate their subject and expand audience perceptions of what documentary can be.

ASIF KAPADIA

Top: *Senna* (2010)
Bottom: *Amy* (2015)

INTRODUCTION

Since its inception, cinema has documented the world around us. The earliest surviving moving image, employing a single lens camera and a strip of paper film, was shot by French artist and filmmaker Louis Le Prince in October 1888. With a duration of just 2.11 seconds, *Roundhay Garden Scene* recorded Prince's family at play. Seven years later, in December 1895, Auguste and Louis Lumière screened ten single-shot vignettes of everyday life to a paying audience at the Salon Indien du Grand Café in Paris. The Lumières' described their *cinématographie* programme as 'actuality films'.

The 'actuality' of what the Lumiéres had achieved was deceptive. The first film in the programme, *Workers Leaving the Lumiére Factory* (1895), exists in three versions, shot over different seasons that are reflected in the clothing worn. There is also a structure to these *actualities*; the Lumières were already constructing a simple narrative of daily life within one shot. And the framing perfectly captured what these pioneer filmmakers wanted us to see. What audiences watched was a constructed reality – real life viewed through the prism of a filmmaker's perspective.

By 1903, as films grew in length, scale and complexity, non-fiction cinema was relegated to the periphery. Audiences' desire to be entertained saw narrative cinema dominate. This didn't deter filmmakers intent on capturing life around the world. Some travelled to the extremes of the Earth, bringing previously unseen images of landscapes and life to audiences, from Herbert Ponting's record of Captain Robert Falcon Scott's ill-fated 1912 journey to the South Pole in *The Great White Silence* (1924) or Frank Hurley's account of a later attempt by Sir Ernest Shackleton in *South* (1919) to Robert Flaherty's *Nanook of the North* (1922, p.160). Flaherty's film marked an early entry in the broad spectrum of ethnographic filmmaking – predominantly Western filmmakers' perspectives on non-Western societies – whose key figures included

Above: *Workers Leaving the Lumiére Factory* (1895)

9

Margaret Mead, John Marshall and Jean Rouch. Some of these filmmakers produced work that blurred the distinction between non-fiction and narrative cinema ('docu-fiction'), which not only raised concerns regarding representation but questioned the parameters of the term 'documentary'.

The first use of that word appeared in a review of Flaherty's 1926 film *Moana*, which captured life on the Polynesian island of Samoa. John Grierson, writing in the *New York Sun*, described the film as having 'documentary value'. In heightening the 'reality' of what he was filming, combining staged scenes with moments free of any 'direct' manipulation, Flaherty sought to give audiences a greater understanding of the world they were witnessing. Even documentaries that don't employ staged scenes, where the filmmaker points a camera and records what unfolds before the lens, the audience is still subject to a specific perspective. Alfred Hitchcock once noted in a conversation with the French filmmaker François Truffaut, 'In the documentary the basic material has been created by God, whereas in the fiction film the director is God; he must create life.' The documentary filmmaker still chooses how to present this 'basic material' and edit it together. Nowhere is this more apparent than in propaganda filmmaking. Soviet and Nazi governments quickly identified the power of film to sway the masses, albeit through the adoption of two very different approaches. Former

Below: *Moana* (1926)

actor Leni Riefenstahl led the vanguard in lionising Hitler's vision of Germany. Her *Triumph of the Will* (1935) and *Olympia* (1938) were technically audacious, emphasizing scale and the Nazi's obsession with racial purity, within the conventions of a linear narrative. The work of Soviet filmmakers and theorists such as Dziga Vertov, Lev Kuleshov, Esfir Shrub, Victor Turin and Sergei Eisenstein lay in a more radical form of cinema. Soviet montage theory placed greater emphasis on the editing process. If each shot conveyed a specific meaning, the combination of two or more shots could create an additional level of meaning. What these directors achieved would influence subsequent generations of narrative, documentary and experimental filmmakers.

Between the emergence of the Soviet filmmakers of the 1920s and the Nazi's establishment of the Ministry of Propaganda in 1933, another major documentary movement was established in the UK. In late 1927, director, writer and critic John Grierson took up a role as a film officer for the Empire Marketing Board, moving in the early 1930s – with his assembled group of filmmakers – to the General Post Office (GPO). A champion of Flaherty's work and greatly enamoured by the pioneering Soviet filmmakers (although he stated a preference for the less radically experimental work produced by them), Grierson saw the utilitarian and educational value of documentary: 'I look on cinema as a pulpit, and use it as a propagandist'. His own 1929 film *Drifters*, about the North Sea herring fishery reflected this. With the GPO Film Unit, he helped forge a style of informative documentary that proved influential in its era and beyond. His team, including Paul Rotha, Basil Wright, Harry Watt, Alberto Cavalcanti and Humphrey Jennings, defined the British Documentary Film Movement. And films like *Coal Face* (1935), *Night Mail* (1936, p.211), *The Saving of Bill Blewitt* (1936) and *London Can Take It!* (1940) balanced grittiness with lyricism.

The outbreak of the Second World War saw propaganda filmmaking increase. The GPO Film Unit was morphed into the Crown Film Unit, which was part of the British government's Ministry of Information. (By this time, Grierson had moved across the Atlantic and headed up the equally influential National Film Board of Canada.) Other Allied countries followed suit. In the US, Hollywood directors such as John Ford, William Wyler, John Huston, George Stevens and Frank Capra all turned their attention to producing propaganda. Some, like Ford and Huston, joined forces on the front line, while others corralled footage into rousing accounts of life, from the domestic front to the battle line.

From the 1920s to the end of the 1940s, documentary production expanded around the globe. But information regarding its development throughout many countries during this period is sketchy at best. Likewise, the role of women in documentary cinema has too often lacked the recognition they deserve. From Esfir Shrub and Yelizaveta Svilova to Marion Grierson, Jenny Gilbertson and Jill Craigie, female filmmakers were producing an essential body of work, often against greater barriers than their male peers. Recent years have seen national film archives start to redress these issues, but many films, both landmark works and examples of a developing style or theme, remain difficult to see.

The importance of propaganda filmmaking during the Second World War saw significant investment in the development of lighter equipment. By the 1950s, a generation of filmmakers emerged who envisaged a new kind of documentary. Just as the French New Wave challenged conservatism in narrative cinema, so a nascent movement of directors in France, the US and the UK challenged the traditions of the documentary form. Direct Cinema in the US, the Free Cinema movement in the UK and cinema vérité in France all embraced mobile technology and aimed to capture reality as 'truthfully' as they could. *Primary* (1960, p.58) and *Chronicle of a Summer* (1961, p.20) led the charge.

Just as television appeared to pose an existential threat to the future of mainstream narrative cinema from the 1950s on, the small screen also changed the way many documentaries were consumed. Although some features continued to be made for theatrical exhibition, the majority of documentaries were produced for television, either as standalone works or in serial form. Like their cinematic counterparts, television documentaries ran the gamut in terms of form, style and content. Another new generation of filmmakers emerged. Some would move into feature documentary filmmaking, while others excelled within the parameters of small-screen production.

The 2000s has seen a significant increase in the popularity of theatrical documentaries. Key social and political issues, from the 'War on Terror' to the environment, have attracted audiences. Some films have experienced unprecedented critical attention and commercial success. Polemical filmmaker Michael Moore's *Bowling for Columbine* (2002) enjoyed a healthy box office, while his next film, *Fahrenheit 9/11* (2004), attracted success on a par with a blockbuster feature.

The 2000s also saw the aesthetics and accessibility of documentaries radically change. Digital technology made filmmaking more mobile, while subsequent improvements and innovations have given even the lowest-budget productions a 'cinematic' quality. Meanwhile, the proliferation of streaming services has significantly increased audience access to documentaries. Many older films are now more widely available, while new feature and serial documentaries have seen their appeal broaden. Moira Demos and Laura Ricciardi's *Making a Murderer* (2015–18, p.198) was not only a successful series, it became a cultural phenomenon.

Casting a net across a wide range of feature, television and serial documentaries, *Well Documented* comprises 100 entries, alongside an overview of 20 key short films (less than 45 minutes in length). Further context is supplied by links between entries listed in the book. And each of the 100 entries is accompanied by recommendations of other films to watch, contextualized by filmmaker, topic, theme and/or style. An attempt has been made to encompass as wide a range of films as possible, from the earliest documentary features to the most recent, as well as entries from a wide variety of countries, and diverse group of artists and filmmakers. Some embraced a classical narrative structure, while others experiment in ways that highlight how the form has developed.

Above: *Bowling for Columbine* (2002)

Divided into six thematic chapters, the book balances well-known or critically acclaimed films with entries that have received less attention, become unduly forgotten, or are more recent additions to the genre. The themes of each chapter are wide and intended to cross over. *O.J.: Made in America* (2016, p.200) appears in Crime and Injustice, but its engagement with American society at large could find it sitting just as easily in Politics and Society. Likewise, Agnés Varda's sense of wonder at the process of creation places *The Gleaners and I* (2000, p.106) in Art and Culture, but its focus on the individuals she encounters on her journey could see it located in People and Places. The themes are a starting point in exploring the worlds each film navigates.

This book is not intended to be an exhaustive history of documentary filmmaking. Nor is it a listing of the best and most popular documentaries ever made. However, a glance at critics' lists of the greatest documentaries, or box-office results for non-fiction film, will feature many titles that are included here, either covered in detail or as additional entries to seek out. What this book ultimately aims to show is that the term used to define these films is not limited to one style or practice. Documentary encompasses the most intimate reflections and wider portraits of societies at large. Its camera can be a fly-on-the-wall or an extension of the filmmaker's personality. The films can be shot on the hoof or composed with a painterly eye. They can reflect the moment in which they were made or edge towards abstraction. Documentary should be seen less as a limiting term than a way of describing an approach to filmmaking whose boundaries are limitless. The titles in this book hopefully go some way to showing just how wide-ranging it can be.

PEOPLE &

PLACES

MAN WITH A MOVIE CAMERA

CHELOVEK S KINO-APPARATOM
DZIGA VERTOV; SOVIET UNION;
1929; 68 MINS

Dziga Vertov was instrumental in forging a radical new form of cinema. Born David Abelevich Kaufman, he believed in the creation of 'a truly international absolute language of cinema based on its complete separation from the language of theatre and literature'. *Man with a Movie Camera* is the distillation of his thoughts and experiments regarding the possibilities of film. And Vertov's emergence, like so many of his filmmaker peers, is bound to the revolution that saw Russia transform from a feudal nation into a Communist state.

The film opens with an audience taking their seats in a cinema, before six chapters record a day in the life of a city. (Footage was shot in Moscow and the Ukrainian cities of Kyiv, Kharkiv and Odessa, although they are presented as one metropolis.) The camera operator is as important a character as the subjects he shoots, frequently appearing on screen, sometimes to set-up a shot. Likewise, a brief interlude cuts to an editor (Vertov's wife Yelizaveta Svilova) piecing individual shots together. Alongside the succession of images that capture the frenetic activity of urban life, Vertov keeps us aware of the process of creation, while also realizing the film's propagandist role of celebrating Lenin and Stalin's project of modernization, enshrining life in a Soviet city, at rest, work and play.

Vertov, alongside fellow pioneer Sergei Eisenstein, helped forge the theoretical framework of montage – a style of filmmaking that employed editing as an ideological tool, with a series of shots conveying meaning beyond that of each individual shot. Where as Eisenstein employed this radical technique – which stands in stark contrast to the seamless, 'invisible' editing of classical Hollywood films – in fiction films like *Battleship Potemkin* (1925), Vertov remained committed to non-fiction and finding new ways to represent the world around him. Freely associating images, *Man with a Movie Camera* employs jump-cuts, stop-motion animation, slow-motion and a variety of other techniques to conjure up a vision of a world in motion. Nearly a century on, Vertov's achievement still feels radical, pushing the envelope of editing techniques, and revelling in the possibilities of film.

ALSO SEE

À Propos de Nice
(p.210)

Berlin: Symphony of a Great City
(Walter Ruttmann; 1927)
A day in the life of the German capital.

Enthusiasm
(Dziga Vertov; 1930)
A bracing account of USSR's radical programme of industrialization.

London
(Patrick Keiller; 1994)
A year in the life of the titular city, seen through the perspective of a fictional narrator.

I AM THE CINE-EYE.
I AM THE MECHANICAL EYE.

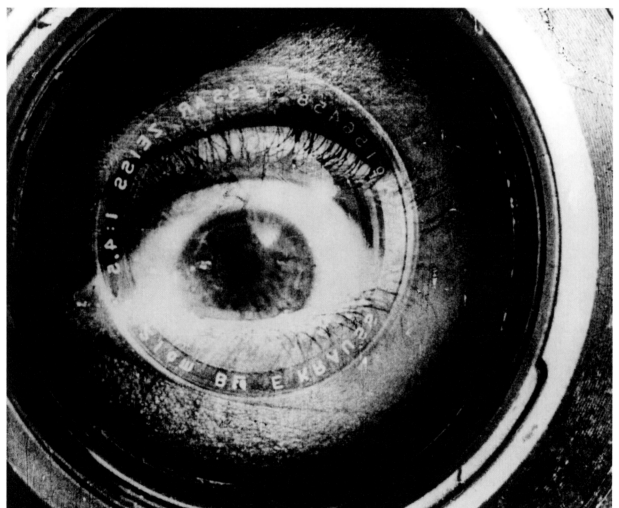

I THE MACHINE SHOW YOU THE WORLD AS ONLY I CAN SEE IT.

Dziga Vertov

ARAYA

MARGOT BENACERRAF;
VENEZUELA/FRANCE;
1959; 90 MINS

Margot Benacerraf's sole feature is a portrait of human existence on a remote coastline of Venezuela. Echoing the ethnographic style of Robert Flaherty, the film focuses on a small community of labourers who live adjacent to the region's vast salt pan marshes and subsist through the backbreaking work of harvesting the mineral for export.

In the film's prologue, a voiceover describes the Araya peninsula as a place of 'desolation, wind and sun' informing us that from 'the marriage of the sea and the sun, salt was born'. Human presence significantly increased in the sixteenth century when the price of salt made places like Araya veritable goldmines. But the only evidence of the first few centuries of occupation in the film are the ruins of a fortress; once impenetrable by enemy forces, the elements have reduced it to rubble.

Apart from a brief epilogue hinting at the mass industrialization that is destined to change life in the region, *Araya* mostly focuses on the peasants whose existence has remained the same for centuries, contrasting their struggle with the desolate beauty of the world around them. Shot in crisp, lustrous monochrome, contrasting the blanched landscape against the ebb and occasionally turbulent flow of the sea, Benacerraf structured her film around a single day, with families repeating the same routine throughout the year. Those working on the salt pyramids – mountains of the mineral that await transportation and export – start before dawn. The salt is sifted for impurities, carried on to the pyramids and bagged into hemp sacks. On the shore, some are engaged in fishing – the only source of nutritious food in the region – while further inland others make pots and tools, or collect fresh water, which has to be transported by truck to each of the small communities in the region. And at night, while most families sleep, another group rows into the salt marshes, cutting out lumps ready to be dried and gathered the next day.

The voiceover, present throughout the film, is more of a tone poem than elucidatory narration, distancing us from the inner lives of the villagers. Likewise, Benacerraf's directorial style revels in the details of physical activity over psychological or emotional engagement with her subjects. Some critics were dismissive of Benacerraf's approach, although French filmmaker Jean Renoir was stunned by her achievement and advised her, 'don't cut a single image'. The film premiered at the Cannes Film Festival, where it shared the Critics' Prize with Alain Resnais' *Hiroshima, mon amour*.

ALSO SEE

Manufactured Landscapes
(p.173)

Salt for Svanetia
(Mikhail Kalatozov; 1930)
A portrait of a rural community in Georgia, where salt is scarce.

Man of Aran
(Robert Flaherty; 1934)
A semi-fictional documentary of life in a community living on the island off the west coast of Ireland.

People from Praia da Vieira
(António Campos; 1975)
An ethnographic portrait of a Portuguese fishing village.

CHRONICLE OF A SUMMER

CHRONIQUE D'UN ÉTÉ
EDGAR MORIN, JEAN ROUCH;
FRANCE; 1961; 125 MINS

ALSO SEE

El Sopar
(p.60)

Moi, un noir
(Jean Rouch; 1958)
This controversial portrait of
Nigerian migrants seeking work
on the Ivory Coast influenced
the French New Wave.

Le Joli Mai
(Chris Marker; 1963)
The filmmaker takes to the streets
of Paris to ask its citizens
questions about their lives.

Love Meetings
(Pier Paolo Pasolini; 1965)
The poet and filmmaker takes to the
Italian streets to find out what people
think – and know – about sex.

Chronicle of a Summer opens with a voiceover telling us: 'This film was made without actors, but lived by men and women who devoted some of their time to a novel experiment, of "film-truth".' Comprising interviews recorded with students and workers over the course of one summer, the film – and the philosophy behind it – consciously acknowledges the active role played by filmmakers in the creative process, even featuring them on screen.

Following the release of *Primary* (1960, p.58) and the emergence of Direct Cinema in the US, ethnofiction filmmaker Jean Rouch and philosopher Edgar Morin conceived the notion of cinéma vérité ('film-truth') with this innovative documentary. The term is a direct reference to Russian filmmaker Dziga Vertov's application of it in his filmmaking process ('Kino-Pravda'), wherein a deeper truth can be caught on camera that might be missed by the human eye. In this instance, it involved a series of interviews carried out by the filmmakers and their associates that presents a barometer of life in France at the beginning of what would become a turbulent decade.

Chronicle of a Summer continued Rouch's experimentation with form, which had dominated his work over the previous decade, while Morin gave the director a structure to work with – combining on-the-street vox-pop questionnaires ('Are you happy?') with more in-depth discussions among students, academics and workers. The topics ranged from the personal to the political; in one scene a worker discusses the challenges of life in a factory; in another an Italian émigrée talks candidly about her feelings of loneliness. Race and colonialization are constants in group discussions – the conflict in French-occupied Algeria was raging at the time – alongside debates over class and workers' rights. In one of the film's most memorable moments, an assistant on the film discusses her Jewish family's experience during the Holocaust, her emotional voiceover accompanying footage of her crossing Place de la Concorde. Inventive throughout, *Chronicle of a Summer* closes with some of the subjects watching a rough cut of the film followed by discussion of what the filmmakers achieved, after which Rouch and Morin briefly reflect on the merits of their enterprise.

The decades since Rouch and Morin conducted their film experiment have witnessed an increasingly mediated society. The interviewees in *Chronicle of a Summer* aren't completely oblivious to the endeavour they're taking part in, but their guilelessness is a world away from the way many now behave in our media-saturated age.

IT'S ONE OF THE GREATEST,
MOST AUDACIOUS,

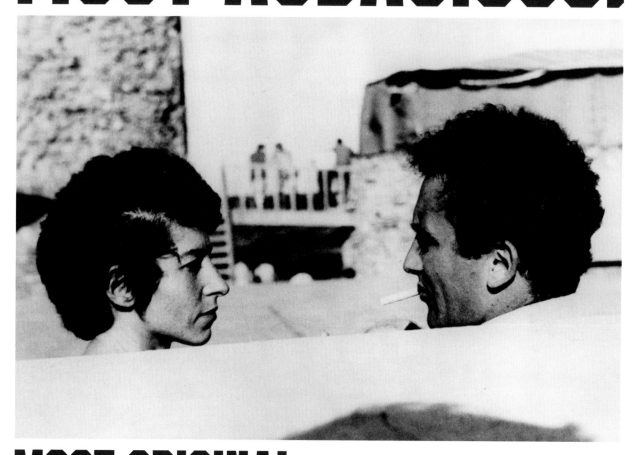

MOST ORIGINAL
DOCUMENTARIES EVER MADE...

I HAD NO IDEA IT WOULD

GO ON AS LONG AS IT DID.

Michael Apted

THE UP SERIES

PAUL ALMOND, MICHAEL APTED;
UK; 1964-2019; 1,019 MINS

ALSO SEE

Ten Minutes Older
(p.214)

People's Century
(Various; 1995–97)
An account of the twentieth century
through the eyes of everyday people.

Minding the Gap
(Bing Liu; 2018)
A skateboarder spent 12 years recording
the lives of his close-knit group of
friends in small-town Illinois.

Recorder: The Marion Stokes Project
(Matt Wolf; 2019)
A portrait of an American woman who
recorded 840,000 hours of television
news footage over four decades.

What began as a one-off portrait of young lives from different backgrounds and locations around the United Kingdom transformed into a landmark documentary series and a barometer of British life over the course of 55 years. As the title of each instalment makes clear, a film crew returned to the subjects every seven years, documenting changes in their lives.

Michael Apted started out as a researcher on *Seven Up!* (1964), taking over as director from Paul Almond in 1970. Initially, he and future theatre director Gordon McDougall were tasked with finding children from a broad spectrum of English life, across class and privilege. They took 20 candidates for a day out at London Zoo, to see how they interacted and behaved on camera. Of those, 14 were eventually chosen for the series. Only four were female, a decision Apted later spoke of with regret.

A TV executive's throwaway comment to Apted about continuing the series prompted the decision to make *7 Plus Seven* (1970). As with subsequent instalments, interviews with each subject were generally shot over two days. Similar questions were posed to each participant, regarding family, class, religion and society, as well as any hopes and concerns they had for the future. The films featured minimal voiceover narration and no accompanying music, with Apted intercutting between the participants. This style attracted occasional criticism for implying meaning that might not have been present in the original interview. But taken together, the films provide a unique record of changing attitudes in English life. In particular, each ensuing film accentuated the problems of class inequality, with the hopes of some children dashed by their circumstances. For others, the pressures of adulthood transformed their view of the world.

Over time, the line-up of interviewees reduced. Charles Furneaux dropped out after *21 Up* (1977). Suzy Lusk didn't appear in *63 Up*. And Lynn Johnson died in 2013, a year after *56 Up* aired. Apted died in 2019, throwing the future of the project into doubt. But a number of long-standing crew members and interviewees have suggested the possibility of one final episode. As Jackie Bassett noted, '70 and 7 do have a good symmetry'. But with their ages, 'it would definitely have to be the last one for everybody'.

TOKYO OLYMPIAD

TŌKYŌ ORINPIKKU
KON ICHIKAWA; JAPAN;
1965; 170 MINS

The Games of the XVIII Olympiad, which took place in and around Tokyo in 1964, were not just the first significant Olympics of the post-Second World War era. They were a symbol of Japan's re-entry upon the world stage, a metaphor for the country's radical process of modernization and a showcase for its technological advancement. Kon Ichikawa's record of the event was also significant for being the first major filmed account of the games since Leni Riefenstahl's *Olympia* (1938), a two-part record of the 1936 Berlin Olympics.

The Japanese Olympics Committee had wanted internationally recognized filmmaker Akira Kurosawa to direct the film. But his demands, including organizing the opening and closing ceremonies, proved too much. Ichikawa, by contrast, was a reliable director who had worked across a variety of genres. And in works like *The Burmese Harp* (1956), *Fires on the Plain* (1959) and *An Actor's Revenge* (1963), his international breakthrough, he mined a vein of humanism that would become a defining aspect of *Tokyo Olympiad*.

In contrast to Riefenstahl, who drew heavily on Greek and Aryan iconography to celebrate physical achievement, Ichikawa chose a more intimate perspective. Following a prologue that briefly details Japan's modernization and captures the excitement of the opening ceremony, Ichikawa's intentions are evident in the way he shoots the men's 100m race. His camera captures athletes in extreme close-up. This style becomes more pronounced in the field events, often edging towards the abstract; shot-putters, hammer throwers and weightlifters are viewed in near-forensic proximity, with the director focusing on faces and body parts. Unlike Riefenstahl, Ichikawa shows more interest in the passion of participation than the celebration of victory. Nowhere is this more evident than in his focus on Chadian runner Ahmed Issa, who is filmed on and off the track, honouring his achievement in reaching the Games even though he fails to win a place in the men's 800m final.

Tokyo Olympiad captures key events of the Games, from the victory of the Japanese women's volleyball team to a gruelling nine-hour struggle between the two finalists in the men's high jump. Some feature in stills, slow motion and black and white. But all reflect Ichikawa's desire to capture the spirit of the film's opening statement, which describes the Games and the athletes' participation as 'a symbol of human aspiration'.

I WANT TO SHOW

Kon Ichikawa

THE SWEAT

PORTRAIT OF JASON

SHIRLEY CLARKE;
US; 1967; 105 MINS

Two years before the Stonewall riots in Manhattan's Greenwich Village prompted a shift in attitudes towards homosexuality that would ripple far beyond New York, Shirley Clarke recorded an interview with a 33-year-old Black gay hustler. What transpired over the course of 12 hours of shooting in Clarke's Chelsea Hotel apartment was a radical project – a film intended for cinema exhibition solely comprising an individual, in close proximity to a camera, talking about their life.

Clarke's subject introduces himself twice, first as Jason Holliday and then, with more than a little amusement, as Aaron Payne. The name change from the latter to the former took place when he moved to the West Coast: 'Jason was created in San Francisco – and San Francisco is a place to be created, believe me.' Mostly sitting, with a glass of spirits in one hand and a cigarette in the other, Jason retraces his life, from a tough childhood and overbearing father, his experiences as a 'Houseboy' to wealthy, elderly white San Franciscans and his friendships with celebrities, to life as a 'stone cold whore' who has 'been balling from Maine to Mexico'. He performs impressions of Fanny Brice and Scarlett O'Hara, even recreates a scene from *Carmen Jones* (1954), and jokes that 'I can fall in and out of love as fast as you can turn on the electric light'. Yet, in his more rueful moments his mask drops – or another emerges – and Jason expresses a loneliness he can't bear and the desire to make a real connection.

Clarke befriended Jason through various acquaintances. (They include Carl Lee, the co-writer with Clarke of her 1963 feature *The Cool World*, who was present during the interview, asking Jason questions and occasionally goading him.) A trained dancer whose film work has often focused on performance and blurred the line between fiction and reality, Clarke keeps us cognizant of the artifice of the enterprise, starting and ending each shot out of focus, and keeping her spoken directions on the soundtrack. The resulting film feels as inspired by the portrait shorts that Andy Warhol manufactured in his Factory as it is by cinéma vérité.

Over half a century later, Jason's 'performance' remains radical. A candid portrait of a complex individual, Clarke's film is a fascinating exploration of the layers people create to cushion themselves from the world and a trailblazing work that presaged the age of confessional television.

ALSO SEE

Geri
(p.104)

Word is Out
(Nancy Adair, Andrew Brown, Rob Epstein; 1977)
A groundbreaking, interview-led documentary in which men and women discuss being gay.

Tongues Untied
(Marlon Riggs; 1989)
A frank portrait of the lives of Black homosexuals in the US.

Gendernauts: A Journey Through Shifting Identities
(Monika Treut; 1999)
An exploration of trans culture and identity in and around San Francisco.

TITICUT FOLLIES

FREDERICK WISEMAN;
US; 1967; 84 MINS

Frederick Wiseman's feature debut is an unvarnished and controversial account of the life of inmates in Massachusetts' Bridgewater State Hospital for the criminally insane. Made in the unobtrusive style that has come to define his five-decade body of work, Wiseman's film highlights his fascination with the bureaucratic nature of social institutions and their interaction with the people and communities they serve.

Prior to *Titicut Follies*, Wiseman's only experience in film was as producer of Shirley Clarke's acclaimed street gang drama *The Cool World* (1963). A law student at Boston University, Wiseman had been involved with Bridgewater from an educational perspective some years before he approached its superintendent to seek permission to film there. After 12 months of negotiations, he received verbal consent, but he and cameraman John Marshall were followed at all times during filming by corrections staff. There was constant assessment of the mental competence of subjects, which restricted what could be filmed. Nevertheless, the footage Wiseman did get proved incendiary.

Bookended by the annual variety show at the institution that gives the film its title, *Titicut Follies* details the severity of the inmates' existence. With few exceptions, staff exhibit indifference or mockery that edges towards bullying, their actions heightening the emotional state of some patients. Bathing is regarded as licence for ritual humiliation; the trauma of the experience writ large on the faces of patients, but blithely ignored by those responsible for their welfare. In another scene, an inmate who has refused to eat, is force fed. The moment is intercut with later footage of the man's corpse being cleaned and his subsequent burial.

Wiseman's film presented such a despairing vision of Bridgewater and its practices that prior to its premiere at the 1967 New York Film Festival, the Massachusetts government attempted to ban it. The screening was allowed, but shortly after a different judge ordered the film destroyed, citing patient privacy over the First Amendment right to free speech. Wiseman (pictured above at a censorship hearing) took the film to the Massachusetts Supreme Judicial Court, who allowed it to be screened to medical professionals only. It wasn't seen by the public until 1991. Nevertheless, it was pivotal in prompting calls for changes to poorly managed psychiatric institutions in the US.

SALESMAN

ALBERT MAYSLES, DAVID
MAYSLES, CHARLOTTE ZWERIN;
US; 1969; 91 MINS

ALSO SEE

Grey Gardens
(p.32)

Meet Marlon Brando
(Albert Maysles, David Maysles; 1966)
The Hollywood star charms his way
through a series of press interviews
for an upcoming film.

Marjoe
(Sarah Kernochan, Howard Smith; 1972)
A former child preacher collaborates
with the filmmakers on an exposé of
the business side of evangelism.

*The Leader, His Driver and
the Driver's Wife*
(Nick Broomfield; 1991)
A disturbing yet often funny portrait
of South African white supremacist
Eugène Terre'Blanche.

This portrait of door-to-door Bible salesmen established Albert and David Maysles as two of the era's most significant documentary filmmakers. Refining the direct cinema style that had become increasingly prevalent since the early 1960s, the film presents a fascinating account of travelling salesmen that draws on the literary spirit of Upton Sinclair, Eugene O'Neill and Arthur Miller. In doing so, it explores a vital aspect of the American Dream; the self-made man.

After garnering praise for a series of documentary shorts, including *Showman* (1963), *Meet Marlon Brando* (1966) and *With Love From Truman* (1966) – the first collaboration to feature Charlotte Zwerin as their principal editor, who is often credited as their co-director – the brothers began looking for a suitable subject for their documentary feature debut. They wanted to prove that direct cinema didn't have to focus on well-known subjects or grapple with high drama; it could easily engage audiences with a snapshot of everyday life. David suggested they choose a salesman, and a recent encounter with an old schoolmate, now a Bible salesman, decided the trade – one that was rich with metaphor. It then took another five months to find the right subject, Paul Brennan, whose combination of huckster charm and defeatism recalls two classic characters from O'Neill and Miller's plays: Hickey from *The Iceman Cometh* and Willy Loman, the doomed protagonist of *Death of a Salesman*.

Brennan, nicknamed 'The Badger', along with his colleagues Charles McDevitt ('The Gipper'), James Baker ('The Rabbit') and Raymond Martos ('The Bull') are seen going house-to-house in New England, selling Bibles to families affiliated to a local church. Each has their own schtick with customers and the air of competitiveness between the men gives their banter an edge. But following a sales meeting full of bravado and a change in location – the team travel to Florida – Brennan's confidence crumbles. His humour becomes bitter and strained. Even his colleagues notice the change in his dealings with potential customers, with McDevitt informing him: 'Paul, you're fighting 'em. They spot it a mile off.'

The Maysles' camera stays close to the men. The film doesn't judge their words or actions, allowing audiences to draw their own conclusions. But the directors' compassion for Brennan is palpable. As *Salesman* ends, his bags are packed and he stands in the doorway to a new life. The humour that once came so easy to him now fails to rise a laugh out of the men he is about to leave for good.

MY BROTHER AND I HAD BOTH BEEN SALESMEN... SO WE UNDERSTOOD THE POTENTIAL OF THE SUBJECT.

Albert Maysles

AN AMERICAN FAMILY

CRAIG GILBERT
(CONCEIVED, PRODUCED);
US; 1973; 720 MINS

ALSO SEE

The *Up* Series
(p.22)

Best Boy
(Ira Wohl; 1979)
An intimate account of the director's
52-year-old cousin Philly, who lives
with his elderly parents.

***Lance Loud!: A Death in
an American Family***
(Alan Raymond, Susan Raymond; 2003)
A moving portrait of the eldest Loud son,
filmed shortly before his death
from AIDS-related illnesses.

Papirosen
(Gastón Solnicki; 2011)
The filmmaker captures a decade in
the life of his extended family.

Can everyday family life be captured truthfully on film, or are the results too affected by the presence of a camera? This was one of many questions raised in the aftermath of PBS screening Craig Gilbert's 12-part series focusing on the Louds, an upper-middle-class family living in Santa Barbara, California. More than just a portrait of one household, the series became the televisual byword for 'the American family' and the inspiration for a wave of fly-on-the-wall – later known as reality – series that followed in its wake.

Between 30 May and 31 December 1971, a film crew entered the eight-room ranch of William and Pat Loud and their five children, Michelle, Delilah, Grant, Kevin and the eldest, Lance, who was living in New York. Over the course of 300 hours of filming, the filmmakers captured a multitude of moments from the family's life; most notably, Lance coming out as gay and Pat announcing that she wanted a divorce from William. If small-screen documentary representations of US domesticity had previously shown families as a cohesive and happy reflection of the American Dream, albeit with the occasional fissure, the Louds were the equivalent of a nuclear meltdown.

For a station normally used to modest audience figures, PBS had a huge hit on its hands. Some praised Gilbert's achievement. The anthropologist and filmmaker Margaret Mead was ecstatic: 'I think it may be as important for our time as were the invention of drama and the novel for earlier generations.' Others – including members of the Loud family – were more dismayed with what Gilbert chose to portray. Although Lance became a minor celebrity, William was upset by what he saw as a negative portrayal of both him and his family.

The question of Gilbert and his crew's presence affecting the behaviour of the Louds on camera was never resolved and remains central to any discussion of this form of filmmaking. The show's runaway success inspired a trend for non-fiction television programming across the world, from the 1974 British version, *The Family*, to *Keeping Up with the Kardashians* (2006–21). By the standards of the modern reality TV show *An American Family* appears tame, but its influence over this genre is impossible to overstate.

OF COURSE, WE'RE ALL PEEPING TOMS

AND SO I SUPPOSE WE SHOULD BE GLAD THAT SOME OF US ARE ALSO EXHIBITIONISTS.

IF WE HAD GOTTEN ONE FRAME OF IT WRONG THEY WOULD HAVE LET US KNOW.

THEY WERE BOUVIERS TO THE CORE.

Albert Maysles

GREY GARDENS

ALBERT MAYSLES, DAVID MAYSLES,
ELLEN HOVDE, MUFFIE MEYER;
US; 1975; 95 MINS

Riding on the wave of critical acclaim for *Salesman* (1969) and *Gimme Shelter* (1970), Albert and David Maysles were approached by Lee Radziwill, the sister of Jackie Kennedy, to make a film about her family. But the project floundered when it came to her eccentric aunt and cousin, both named Edith Bouvier Beale. Radziwill realized her vision of the documentary differed wildly from what the Maysles intended and gave up on the project, confiscating the footage that had been shot. But the Beales were too enticing a subject for the brothers and, under their own steam, they returned to East Hampton, recording hundreds of hours of footage. The result is a marvel of editing and non-linear storytelling, and a pivotal work in the history of documentary.

The film opens with a tone of warm familiarity; Albert and his camera aren't strangers to mother and daughter Edith and Edie Beale. Edith sits on the upper landing of her dilapidated house as Edie searches for one of their many cats. Their dialogue allows us to familiarize ourselves with their vernacular, a pronounced East Coast drawl. Their conversation is also indicative of the structure of the film, mostly comprising reminiscences, heated exchanges, conversations with Albert and the few visitors to the house, and discussions about the property's state of disrepair. These conversations, combined with the intimacy of Albert's camera, gradually draw us into their strange, singular world.

The Maysles' footage was handed to Ellen Hovde, Muffie Meyer and Susan Froemke to piece together. The film eschews a linear trajectory in favour of a fractured stream of minor events, contretemps between mother and daughter, and Edie's love of performance; it resembles a tapestry of two lives lived in a world haunted by the ghosts of former glories.

Critical reaction to *Grey Gardens* was initially divided, with some claiming the Maysles had exploited the Beales. Yet the affection between Albert and his hosts is evident throughout. Edie defended it, arguing that the Maysles 'get the pith of every situation. There is no difference in the way we lead our lives and what you see'. And close to the end of her life, when asked if she had any final words, Edith replied: 'No, it's all in the film.'

NEWS FROM HOME

CHANTAL AKERMAN;
FRANCE/BELGIUM;
1976;85 MINS

ALSO SEE

Dreams of a Life
(p.46)

Walden: Diaries, Notes and Sketches
(Jonas Mekas; 1969)
An experimental record of events
and encounters in the filmmaker's
life between 1964 and 1968.

Diary 1973–1983
(David Perlov; 1983)
A family diary and a record of life
in Israel over the course of a decade.

No Home Movie
(Chantal Akerman; 2015)
Akerman's final film is a moving portrait
of her relationship with her mother.

Following the critical success of her intimate epic *Jeanne Dielman, 23 quai du commerce, 1080 Bruxelles* (1975), Chantal Akerman journeyed to New York. The film she subsequently made, in which letters from her mother are read over elegantly composed shots of Manhattan's streets, contemplates themes of urban alienation, and personal and familial disconnection. It exists in a hinterland between narrative documentary and the avant-garde, articulating feelings of loneliness that many city dwellers experience.

In 1971, aged 21 and inspired by the work of Jean-Luc Godard, Akerman moved to New York to become a filmmaker. Structuralist critical theory was gaining ground at the time and its influence is apparent in her first documentary feature, *Hôtel Monterey* (1972). If the work from her two-year stay didn't fully represent her sense of dislocation from the world, *News From Home*'s combination of her mother's old letters and a more glacial perspective on the city perfectly capture the unease she once felt.

News From Home comprises a series of mostly static shots of varying lengths that capture Manhattan's streets and subway. Opening at dusk, the first few shots find the camera positioned in the middle of a street or avenue, distanced from any human activity. During the third shot, we hear Akerman's voice, reading the letters. They detail minor family incidents and illnesses, tell of money and clothes despatched by post, and the vagaries of everyday life, becoming repetitive and even banal. However, each new missive, combined with the footage – all of which was shot by Akerman when she returned to the city in 1975 – emphasizes profound feelings of alienation. As with the extended shots in *Jeanne Dielman*, duration adds weight to the work. Two 360-degree pans – at night on the edge of a car park and in a subway station – along with an extended tracking shot, filmed from the side window of a car as it journeys up 10th Avenue, interrupt the more formal static shots. And it ends with a symbolic departure, aboard the Staten Island Ferry as it travels away from Manhattan. *News from Home* is an intensely personal film – a cathartic reflection by Akerman on her emotional and psychological state – about life in a frantic and often impersonal metropolis.

IN NEW YORK, I FELT RELIEVED OF THE WEIGHT OF NOT BELONGING

Chantal Akerman

AND AT THE SAME TIME I FELT THAT I DIDN'T BELONG.

SHERMAN'S MARCH

ROSS MCELWEE;
US; 1985; 157 MINS

A brutal military campaign in the last stages of the American Civil War is the starting point for Ross McElwee's journey through the parts of the US he grew up in. His film soon transforms into something far more personal, as he visits battlesites, ruminates on the nature of his relationships and concludes, 'I'm filming my life in order to have a life to film'. He is a roguish journeyman on his own picaresque adventure, whose lineage draws on the tart humour of Mark Twain and the philosophical ruminations of Henry David Thoreau.

In late 1864, Major General William Tecumseh Sherman of the Union Army led 60,000 soldiers on a month-long campaign into Confederate territory, beginning with the destruction of Atlanta and ending in the capture of the port of Savannah. Following a scorched earth policy, they left thousands dead in their wake along a trail that was 60 miles wide and 700 miles long. It proved to be the undoing of the Confederates. But the viciousness with which Sherman carried out his mission made him a reviled figure in the South.

This information, imparted by Richard Leacock – one of the pioneers of direct cinema and a tutor of McElwee's – opens the film. It is immediately followed by a black and white sequence of McElwee pacing back and forth in an empty New York apartment, telling us that his girlfriend Anne has left him for her former lover. These two thematic strands intertwine over the course of the filmmaker's voyage as he meets old girlfriends, embarks on a few new – and unsuccessful – relationships and pictures life in the US through the prism of its past and the eccentricities of those who live in the present.

Potential lovers include an actress hoping to meet Burt Reynolds, a Doomsday-fixated survivalist, a country-singing Mormon, a charismatic pop singer and a linguistics theorist who lives on a deserted island. Through each of these encounters, with McElwee rarely putting down his camera, the film grapples with its director's belief that true love exists, but it has so far eluded him. Combined with his fears of a nuclear conflict – the stuff of his nightmares when loneliness haunts him – McElwee's strange, fascinating, funny and insightful film underpins the importance of individual lives within the grand narratives of history.

ALSO SEE

The Gleaners and I
(p.106)

Nobody's Business
(Alan Berliner; 1996)
The director sifts through both the momentous and seemingly insignificant events in his father's life.

Bright Leaves
(Ross McElwee; 2003)
Starting with a Gary Cooper movie, the filmmaker travels around the Carolinas in order to trace his family's history.

Cameraperson
(Kirsten Johnson; 2016)
The filmmaker collates moments from her personal and professional life for this travelogue and memoir.

PARIS IS BURNING

JENNIE LIVINGSTON;
US; 1990; 71 MINS

ALSO SEE

Portrait of Jason
(p.26)

The Queen
(Frank Simon; 1968)
A behind-the-scenes look at a
pre-Stonewall national drag
competition in New York City.

*The Death and Life of
Marsha P. Johnson*
(David France; 2017)
An investigation into the still-unsolved
1992 death of the trans icon.

The Gospel of Eureka
(Donal Mosher, Michael Palmieri; 2018)
Mx Justin Vivian Bond narrates the story
of an Arkansas town that plays host to a
Christian festival and drag pageant.

A key early entry in the nascent New Queer Cinema movement, Jennie Livingstone's documentary captured a vital moment in New York's ballroom scene as it emerged from the city's cultural underground. Winner of the Grand Jury Prize for Documentary at the 1991 Sundance Film Festival, it has remained a vital – if controversial – record of that era.

Although attitudes to the LGBT community in New York had changed significantly since the Stonewall Riots of 1969, which were followed by the inception of Gay Pride and the introduction of laws protecting LGBT rights, homophobic attacks remained rife. In this environment, the city's ballroom scene offered a safe space. Livingstone was a student in the early 1980s when she first encountered it. She initially recorded a few interviews, which eventually transformed into a seven-year exploration of the world. Her footage of the balls shows African American and Hispanic gay men, drag queens and transgender women competing in a variety of competitions, from catwalk contests to dance-offs. There are categories for dress and dance styles, and rules regarding behaviour – which were regularly, and gleefully, broken. Many of the contestants belonged to 'houses' – intentional families, including surrogate 'parents' who ensure the safety, support and wellbeing of their group. A language was also developed. To 'read' someone was to perfect what performer Dorian Corey describes as 'the real art form of insult'. While 'shading' employs a more subtle strategy: 'I don't tell you you're ugly,' notes Corey, 'but I don't have to tell you because you know you're ugly. That's shade.' Voguing transforms this into physical form, with a dancer's choreography aimed at outshining a rival.

In addition to filming competitions, Livingstone interviewed many of the key figures on the scene and documented a community impacted by AIDS and the constant threat of homophobic violence. (The film's darkest note details the still unsolved murder of charismatic interviewee Venus Xtravaganza.) By the time the film was released, Madonna had embraced voguing and Willi Ninja had become a crossover star.

Some of the participants claimed they felt exploited by Livingstone, although she and her producers did share the film's modest profits with them. Critics have also accused Livingstone of cultural appropriation, a charge she has vehemently opposed. Nevertheless, *Paris is Burning* remains a fascinating time capsule of a vibrant cultural scene and a celebration of the extraordinary individuals who populated it.

CITY

City Symphonies only existed in their purest form for a decade, but their influence has been great. They offered no subject or narrative other than an exploration of a given urban environment – the cities themselves were the characters in each film. Some were critical of city life, while others were awed by the cacophony of everyday activity. And they ran the gamut, from linear narrative to the avant-garde.

Walter Ruttmann's *Berlin: Symphony of a Great City* (1927) is arguably the best-known film of this genre, a frenetic 24 hours in the life of the German capital. *Manhatta* (1921) came earlier, with Modernist photographers Paul Strand and Charles Sheeler capturing the heady, vertiginous experience of New York constantly reaching upwards. This 'world spanned with iron rails' finds its spiritual descendant in D.A. Pennebaker's Kodachrome short *Daybreak Express* (1953, p.212), set aboard an early morning Manhattan-bound train.

SYMPHONIES

Although Dziga Vertov's *Man with a Movie Camera* (1929, p.16) melds four cities into one propulsive metropolis, it shares the day-and-night-in-the-life theme that so many of the City Symphony films embraced. Other films were even more specific. Joris Ivens directed an array of films that captured life in different cities, but none was more sensual than *Rain* (1929), which recorded Amsterdam before, during and after a storm. While Paris was represented by Alberto Cavalcanti's wildly experimental *Nothing But Time* (1926) and George Lacombe's *La Zone* (1928).

Opposite: *Berlin: Symphony of a Great City* (1927)
Below: *Of Time and the City* (2008)

In the south of France, Jean Vigo set a high benchmark for this form with his playful *À Propos de Nice* (1930, p.210), which contrasted the lives of rich and poor with satirical bite. Yet the film was also playful and mischievous, qualities echoed by Agnès Varda in her colourful French Riviera short *Along the Coast* (1958). These attributes are also evident in more recent films, distantly related to the City Symphony, such as Patrick Keiller's *London* (1994), Terence Davies' ode to Liverpool *Of Time and the City* (2008) and Mark Cousins' *I Am Belfast* (2015).

THE BELOVS

BELOVY
VIKTOR KOSSAKOVSKY;
RUSSIA; 1992; 60 MINS

A fascinating and eccentric portrait of rural life in Russia that belies the era in which it unfolds, *The Belovs* focuses on the fractious relationship between Anna Fyodorovna Belova and her constantly inebriated brother Mikhail, who live together on a dilapidated farm. Little happens, beyond the visit of siblings, some heated arguments and the passing of days. But debut director Viktor Kossakovsky's eye for the idiosyncratic and his skill in locating the Belovs' existence within the grander scheme of life brings depth and pathos to the film.

Set in a present that could easily be mistaken for an earlier time, the film opens on Anna as she tends to her property, mithering over the way it has declined. Twice widowed, she rues the day she listened to her mother and turned down a suitor, believing her refusal is a curse that has plagued her life. All she now cares about are her unruly cows and the upkeep of the ramshackle farm. Mikhail, meanwhile, only has time for his dog and a drink. Things pick up when siblings Vasiliy and Sergey arrive. But dinner soon descends into a debate about the virtues of then President Boris Yeltsin. Mikhail takes umbrage with everything his brothers say and voices are raised. Following their departure, Anna chides Mikhail for his behaviour. Later, as he drunkenly falls to the floor, Anna dances through their cottage, her singing accompanied by her brother's snoring.

Kossakovsky's monochrome study combines the intimacy that made *Gunda* (2020), his day-in-the-life portrait of a pig, so fascinating, with a distinctive worldview that he would push to a magisterial scale with his travelogues *¡Vivan las Antipodas!* (2011) and *Aquarela* (2018). The more expansive worldview of the latter films here takes the form of three musical interludes that tip towards the comical. But a sense of the absurd permeates much of the film, from Anna's beloved but unruly cow wreaking havoc on the farm, to her attempts to protect a hedgehog from her dog. These moments contrast with Mikhail's bullying. At one point, he rises from the table, banging his fist on it, his physicality towering over Anna. Kossakovsky cuts the sound for a minute, allowing only the visuals to play out. In a subsequent scene, Anna responds with laughter and tears as she listens to an audio playback of the argument. As the film closes and Anna dances – metaphorically – on her brother's grave, we're in no doubt as to where Kossakovsky's sympathies lie.

KOSSAKOVSKY IS A SEARCHER FOR MOMENTS OF ECSTATIC OBSERVATION

THAT TRANSFORM ORDINARY INTO CINEMA.

Filmmaker Robert Greene

TO BE AND TO HAVE

ÊTRE ET AVOIR
NICOLAS PHILIBERT;
FRANCE; 2002; 104 MINS

Nicolas Philibert had a breakout hit with this understated and charming film. Ensconced in the small classroom of a primary school in the commune of Saint-Étienne-sur-Usson, close to the Alps in the picturesque French department of Puy-de-Dôme, he recorded a year in the life of the young pupils and their warm, dedicated and generous teacher Georges Lopez. In its quietly ruminative way, *To Be and to Have* reminds audiences of the essential role teachers play in children's lives – nurturing, encouraging and helping them to deal with the world around them.

With a population of around 200, the local community has just one primary school class that caters for ages ranging from four to 12. The children are separated by age across three tables, with Mr Lopez dividing his time between each. The film opens after the first term has begun, with the youngest class mostly familiar with the day-to-day activities. The weather signals progress through the year, from the opening shot of farmers corralling cattle in a blizzard to the arrival of summer and a cutaway to a field of hay bales that resembles a landscape by Millet.

Each small classroom drama, quietly observed, draws out the personality of the children. None more so than Jojo, whose combination of guilelessness and mischievousness, particularly in his attempts to make the most of the school's photocopier, is a joy to watch. Philibert's camera never feels confined within the limited space of the classroom; he cuts between wider shots of the group and close-ups of the pupils in discussion with their teacher, or caught up in their own worlds as they carry out a variety of assignments.

ALSO SEE

Svyato
(p.216)

Around the Village Green
(Marion Grierson, Evelyn Spice; 1937)
An evocation of pastoral life
in England just prior to the
Second World War.

In the Land of the Deaf
(Nicolas Philibert; 1992)
A vivid portrait of life for the hearing
impaired and deaf, from
schoolchildren to the elderly.

Mr Bachmann and His Class
(Maria Speth; 2021)
A schoolteacher makes himself an
invaluable oasis of calm in the
turbulent lives of his pupils.

Philibert visits the homes of some students, witnessing their interaction with family members as they strive to complete their coursework. There is also a journey to a nearby middle school – an adventurous day out for the younger pupils, and for the few older students a snapshot of what the next year holds. The importance of these scenes, particularly two intimate moments in which Mr Lopez consoles and advises two older students, not only highlight the teacher's importance to this small community, but his essential role in these children's lives. Philibert's camera never intrudes, but remains close enough to observe the candour and compassion this remarkable teacher directs towards his charges.

TOUCHING THE VOID

KEVIN MACDONALD;
UK/US; 2003; 106 MINS

The Oscar-winning director of *One Day in September* (1999) transforms a climbing accident into an enthralling and visually striking tale of human endurance. Kevin Macdonald's cliff-edge account of Joe Simpson and Simon Yates' fateful 1985 expedition to the Peruvian Andes skilfully combines dramatic re-enactment with the climbers' own recollections.

Simpson and Yates' ascent along the previously unclimbed west face of the 21,000-feet peak Siula Grande was gruelling, but achieved with little incident. However, on their descent they faced rapidly worsening conditions. Simpson fell and landed badly on his right leg, sending his shin bone up through his knee socket and splitting his femur lengthways. Then, as Yates was lowering him down the mountain by rope, Simpson fell off a ledge. Believing his climbing partner was dead and in an attempt to survive himself, Yates cut the rope – an act for which he felt profound guilt but which Simpson has always defended. It sent Simpson tumbling hundreds of feet down a crevasse. Miraculously, both made it back to base camp.

Macdonald returned with the climbers to Siula Grande to film some distance shots of them, while actors Brendan Mackey and Nicholas Aaron play them in the film's dramatic close-up sequences. These were then intercut with testimonies by the two climbers, along with that of Richard Hawking, who met them on their journey to the mountain and agreed to watch over their belongings at base camp.

Macdonald frames his interviewees in extreme close-up, which only intensifies the horror of their story as they recount it. And as the men describe their worsening situation, the filmmaker's dramatic recreations become more impressionistic, shifting focus from the precariousness of their physical health to their deteriorating psychological condition. The scenes of a dehydrated Simpson constantly hearing running water, or his inability to get a pop song he can't stand out of his head, attain a surreal, dreamlike quality, capturing his confused, fearful and delirious state. These moments are accentuated by Macdonald's use of a SnorriCam – a camera rigged to the body of an actor that adds a layer of disorientation to a shot. The director also makes good use of a layered soundscape and Alex Jeffes' score, emphasizing the peril the men endured and survived, but also evoking the majesty of the peaks that Simpson and Yates would continue to climb for years after these events took place.

MURDERBALL

HENRY ALEX RUBIN, DANA ADAM SHAPIRO; US; 2005; 88 MINS

The competition narrative documentary received an electric jolt via this account of the gladiatorial battle between the US and Canada in the violent world of wheelchair rugby. Unfolding between the 2002 World Cup final and the 2004 Athens Paralympics, *Murderball* balances portraits of the leading figures of the competition with visceral footage from the matches to produce a white-knuckle record of a full-contact sport and the individuals who give their all for it.

The film takes its title from the original name of a sport devised by Canadian wheelchair athletes Gerry Terwin, Duncan Campbell, Randy Dueck, Paul LeJeune and Chris Sargent in 1976. Quad rugby, as it is known in the US, has become an internationally recognized sport and is played by teams from over 25 countries. It's a brutal, hard-contact combination of wheelchair basketball, ice hockey, handball and rugby union. One of its luminaries is Joe Soares. Ruthlessly competitive, he attracted controversy for becoming the Canadian coach after he was dropped from the US team in 1996 and looms large over *Murderball*. However, he faces stiff opposition from the US team, whose most charismatic figure is Mark Zupan. His animosity towards Soares heightens the tension between the two teams following a US defeat, their first at a world championship.

Between the matches, the film details the men's histories and their day-to-day lives, including an hilarious conversation between four US players about sex and the techniques they employ. The players are frank about the challenges they face and passionate in discussing their sport. Nowhere is this more evident than in an exchange between Zupan and Keith Cavill, who only recently damaged his spinal cord in a motorcycle accident and to whom the murderball star conveys a picture of a rich and fulfilled life.

However, the core of the film lies in the game, with both teams giving their all for Olympic Gold. In contrast to the more conventional domestic scenes, the matches are filmed in extreme close-up, with cameras attached to reinforced wheelchairs that resemble chariots. Played out to an industrial metal soundtrack, these bouts highlight Zupan, his team and their adversaries' desire to overcome extraordinary odds in order to live life on their terms.

ALSO SEE

Learning to Skateboard in a Warzone (If You're a Girl)
(p.217)

Spellbound
(Jeffrey Blitz; 2002)
One of the most successful competition narrative documentaries, which revolves around a national spelling bee.

Benda Bilili!
(Renaud Barret, Florent de la Tullaye; 2010)
A portrait of Kinshasa street band Staff Benda Bilili, whose members are survivors of polio.

We Are Poets
(Daniel Lucchesi, Alex Ramseyer-Bache; 2011)
An English slam poetry group prepares to enter the world's most prestigious competition, Brave New Voices.

DREAMS OF A LIFE

CAROL MORLEY; UK/IRELAND;
2011; 95 MINS

On 25 January 2006, the body of Joyce Carol Vincent was found in her north London apartment, above a busy shopping mall. The 38-year-old had been dead for almost three years. Carol Morley's film questions how, when we are more inter-connected than ever, this could have happened. It investigates Joyce's life and the period leading up to her disappearance through dramatic reconstruction and the testimonies of former friends.

Morley first heard of Joyce from a story about her death in a national newspaper. Struck by the portrait it painted of her, particularly the lack of any details, Morley spent the next five years investigating Joyce's life. She placed ads in newspapers and on a London taxi, asking those who knew Joyce to contact her. Gradually some came forward, but the picture of Joyce that emerged seemed in stark contrast to her fate. At one time, she enjoyed an active social life and a close family. She worked constantly and at various points had met or socialized with Stevie Wonder, Gil Scott-Heron and was even filmed at an event with Nelson Mandela.

Employing staged reconstructions featuring actor Zawe Ashton, Morley gradually pieces together Joyce's life. Key to this is friend and one-time partner Martin. (Joyce's four sisters were also in contact with Morley, but chose not to appear in the film.) He movingly describes her personality, ebullience and love of others' company – elements that seem so at odds with the woman who died alone, apparently of natural causes, with her television on and surrounded by Christmas presents for people she was never to see. A sudden disappearance might have sparked greater concern from people who knew her. Instead, with no one knowing where she lived in the last months of her life, Joyce gradually receded from the world. Attempts were made to find her, but with no success.

Morley's film can only speculate what drove Joyce to cut herself off from the world, but it is rightly pained at the course her life took. Ultimately, *Dreams of a Life* is a moving epitaph to a lost soul, whose memory is deserving of more than a sensational tabloid headline.

IT'S A STORY THAT CONFRONTS YOU WITH WHAT IT MEANS TO LIVE NOWADAYS

AND HOW NOTICED WE REALLY ARE.

Carol Morley

STORIES WE TELL

SARAH POLLEY;
CANADA; 2012; 108 MINS

For her first documentary, actor-turned-filmmaker Sarah Polley trained her camera upon her own family's recent past. In particular, she focuses on the relationship between her parents and the events that led to her conception. If stories of family life have long proven rich terrain in drama and documentary, Polley's is all the more compelling for the way she has chosen to tell it.

The film opens with a quote by Margaret Atwood: 'When you're in the middle of a story it isn't a story. It's a confusion.' With it, Polley acknowledges the convoluted nature of her parents' private lives. Her mother Diane met her father Michael when both were actors. They settled down, had two children, and realized they were very different people by the time their third, Sarah, was born. A couple of years later, following a brief battle with cancer, Diane died. A comment regarding Sarah's appearance by one of her siblings – noting how different she looked to them – led her to investigate her mother's life around the time she was conceived, when Diane had briefly taken leave of the family and returned to the theatre. Polley's discovery is what prompted her to make the film. And as revelations about Diane's past surfaced, Michael wrote his daughter a detailed, frank and moving letter, which she has him narrate for the film.

Rather than supplementing the various interviews with archive footage, Polley chose to dramatize her family's past. These sequences – little more than fleeting snapshots – are richly evocative, important more for their tonal quality than for recalling any specific events. But they do establish Diane as a significant presence in the film, beyond the testimonies of friends and family members. They also beg us to question the veracity of the story being told.

ALSO SEE

Sherman's March
(p.36)

Intimate Stranger
(Alan Berliner; 1991)
Berliner explores the extraordinary life of his maternal grandfather.

Katatsumori
(Naomi Kawase; 1994)
The first part of an intimate trilogy by the filmmaker about her grandmother, who raised her.

Surfwise
(Doug Pray; 2007)
A portrait of surfer and physician Dorian 'Doc' Paskowitz and the unconventional life he and his family led.

At one point in the film, Polley films a discussion with a figure who only recently entered her life. He questions her right to tell a part of the story that he feels is his. Even her father notes of the film she has embarked on, 'your editing of this will turn it into something completely different'. Polley's inclusion of these moments acknowledges the extremely subjective nature of filmmaking and storytelling, and that whatever 'truth' is presented it is defined by the perspective of those telling it. As such, *Stories We Tell* is unique for the way that Polley employs film as a means to consolidate the past and find a way through the present.

HALE COUNTY THIS MORNING, THIS EVENING

RAMELL ROSS;
US; 2018; 76 MINS

In 2009, RaMell Ross took up a position as a photography teacher and basketball coach at a school in Hale County, Alabama. Soon after, he began filming life there, the images he captured forming this visual tapestry. Though primarily focused on two young men from the youth programme Ross organized, the film widens its scope across generations. Creating a cinematic language that is all its own, *Hale County This Morning, This Evening* is, by turns, euphoric, painterly and wistful.

Hale County possesses a rich visual history. The photographer Walker Evans and writer James Agee visited the area in 1936, during the Great Depression. Their study of poor white sharecroppers was published in 1941 as *Let Us Now Praise Famous Men*. Ross' film can be seen as a rejoinder to that work, but also a contemporary extension of it, with its focus trained on Black lives. Central to this world are Quincy and Daniel. Quincy lives with Boosey – who is expecting twins – and their child Kyrie. He works at the local catfish processing plant alongside Daniel's troubled mother Mary. Daniel is attending Selma University and hopes to go pro in basketball. It's his chance to escape this world. Ross further populates his film with fragments of daily life, from people at church, socializing at home, or just hanging out on the streets.

Ross captures moments of hope, joy, regret, pain and grief. Others possess an abstract quality that transcends surface meaning to achieve a radiance and beauty; a neon cross shimmering in the night; dusk seen from a moving car; a thunderstorm begins as three girls sing Etta James' 'I'd Rather Go Blind'; shafts of light slicing through tree branches and the smoke of burning tyres. At one point Ross cuts to a clip from *Lime Kiln Club Field Day* (1913), the oldest surviving film to feature African American actors. He then shows the man burning the tyres, who acknowledges Ross' presence, telling him, 'We need more Black folk in the area taking pictures'. *Hale County This Morning, This Evening* is not only a response to that man's suggestion, it also offers a fresh way of looking at the world.

ALSO SEE

Hoop Dreams
(p.68)

Below Sea Level
(Gianfranco Rosi; 2008)
A five-year account of a community eking out an existence in the Californian desert.

What You Gonna Do When the World's on Fire?
(Roberto Minervini; 2018)
A portrait of life for a Black community in New Orleans as Black Lives Matter is gaining traction in the US.

Ascension
(Jessica Kingdon; 2021)
A tapestry of Chinese life whose focus journeys from menial workers through to the country's elite.

DICK JOHNSON IS DEAD

KIRSTEN JOHNSON;
US; 2020; 89 MINS

When Kirsten Johnson's father was diagnosed with dementia, she faced the reality that someone who played an enormous role in her life would soon no longer be a part of it. To grapple with the inevitability of his demise Johnson made a film in which her father dies via a variety of grisly scenarios. The result is a frank contemplation of mortality, an act of remembering and a tender portrait by the filmmaker of her father. Challenging the conventions of the documentary form through its use of staged sequences alongside interactions between the Johnsons, *Dick Johnson is Dead* is often moving, irreverent and very funny.

The idea for the film came to Johnson in a dream. She saw her father lying dead in a coffin before suddenly coming to life and announcing, 'I'm Dick Johnson and I'm not dead yet'. From there, the filmmaker approached her father with the idea of staging his death as a way for both of them to deal with the inevitable. At that point, Richard Johnson, a recently retired clinical psychiatrist, was going through a series of significant life changes in order to cope with his condition. He had lost his driver's licence and was moving out of the home he had shared with his deceased wife, Katie Jo, to be closer to his daughter. But he embraced the film's premise and, over the course of the production, he dies from a falling object, falling down a staircase and having his jugular sliced open. He also makes an appearance in the afterlife, where he is serenaded by his heavenly hosts.

Kirsten Johnson's previous film *Cameraperson* (2016) was a strikingly original memoir constructed through unused footage culled from other film projects – she is a noted cinematographer – along with footage of her family, including Richard and Katie Jo, whose own dementia at the time was severe. *Dick Johnson is Dead* is no less profound. The moments where father and daughter contemplate his condition, the physical and mental limitations affecting a man who once led a full life, are often painful. But they are never exploitative. And the film's final scenes, an emotional rollercoaster culminating in the ritual of memorial, give the last, generous laugh to Richard Johnson, who lives though his own death with exuberance and a wicked, infectious glee.

ALSO SEE

The Act of Killing
(p.150)

Without Memory
(Hirokazu Koreeda; 1996)
A portrait of a man unable to form recent memories after a medical procedure left him with anterograde amnesia.

Kingdom of Us
(Lucy Cohen; 2017)
An intimate record of seven siblings, four of whom are autistic, coming to terms with the suicide of their father.

Some Kind of Heaven
(Lance Oppenheim; 2020)
An account of life in America's largest retirement community, The Villages, in Florida.

A SECRET LOVE

CHRIS BOLAN;
US; 2020; 81 MINS

Terry Donahue and Pat Henschel have lived together as spinsters since the 1950s. At least, that's how their families and acquaintances regarded their existence. In truth, they fell in love almost immediately, were lovers soon after and weren't so much keeping their relationship a secret from the world as judiciously choosing who would know the reality of their life together. In his celebratory film, Chris Bolan, Terry's great nephew, journeys back to the women's early lives to chart the development of their relationship. What emerges is a loving portrait of two people dedicated to each other, in a society that was often far less accepting.

Bolan starts in the present, with Terry having told her beloved niece Diana the truth about her relationship with Pat. Diana accepts the situation without hesitation. Other family members are less happy with what they perceive to be a longstanding untruth. From there, Bolan interviews historians to show how homosexuals and lesbians were treated around the time Terry and Pat became a couple. There is a montage of newspaper clippings detailing 'lurid' stories from the era, alongside footage of a police detective from a Morals and Juvenile squad telling an audience of teenagers: 'One out of three of you will turn queer. And you will be caught. And the rest of your life will be a living hell.'

Terry and Pat kept their 'truth' to a small group of friends. And they lived a full life. Terry was a star player in the All-American Girls Baseball League. They both also played women's ice hockey. In addition to living together, they worked side-by-side for over two decades at an interior design company. Only as Terry's condition – she has Parkinson's – worsens do they find themselves in need of help.

A Secret Love doesn't break new ground as a documentary. Terry and Pat's story is told as a mostly linear journey, featuring highs and lows that comprise the substance of so many lives. But the story of their love for and commitment to each other, their resilience over the years, their decision to live life as they wanted to and, even with the increasing frailty that accompanies old age, their ability to still choose their own destiny, is a joyful sight to behold.

WE'RE JUST LIVING AN ORDINARY LIFE

I DON'T KNOW WHY YOU'D WANT TO FILM IT.

POLITICS

& SOCIETY

PRIMARY

ROBERT DREW & ASSOCIATES;
US; 1960; 53 MINS

Robert Drew's film presented US audiences with a radically different portrait of a political candidate and electoral campaign. It follows Democratic Presidential nominees Hubert H. Humphrey and John F. Kennedy as they canvas voters for the 1960 Wisconsin primary. The film came out at the same time that the French New Wave was rewriting the grammar of fiction cinema. It was the first key work in the influential Direct Cinema movement and would have a seismic impact on documentary filmmaking.

Drew emerged as a filmmaker just as a young generation of filmmakers, including Richard Leacock, Albert and David Maysles, and D.A. Pennebaker, were experimenting with innovations in lightweight camera and sound technology. Leacock had already made the documentary *Toby and the Tall Corn* (1954), whose hand-held camerawork captured intimate moments with apparent ease. Drew approached these filmmakers, along with inventor Mitch Bogdanowicz, who helped develop the mobile equipment they required, to form a production company intent on producing work that challenged the staid conventions of the television documentary at that time. ('Lectures with picture illustrations', as Drew described them.) With *Time-Life* magazine investing in the company, the subject of the group's first film needed to be high-profile enough to gain attention, which is why Drew turned to the race between the traditional Humphrey and Kennedy, the handsome rising star of the Democratic Party.

Primary was a revelation. With minimal voiceover narration, the film captures the two campaigns with a sense of urgency, thanks to its on-the-ground, as-it-happened style. Maysles' celebrated sequence following Kennedy into a hall of ecstatic supporters, and the cut from Jacqueline Kennedy speaking to an audience to a shot of her hands that hints at her nervousness, underpin the way the film positioned itself at the heart of the action. It also caught a key moment in the changing nature of political campaigning, with the youthful Kennedy a more relaxed television presence than Humphrey.

The future president was so impressed with reactions to the film that he collaborated with Drew on two more productions, *Adventures on the New Frontier* (1961) and *Crisis* (1963). The group that made *Primary* disbanded within a few years, but each would have a significant impact on the trajectory of documentary filmmaking over subsequent decades.

ALSO SEE

Salesman
(p.28)

The War Room
(Chris Hegedus,
D.A. Pennebaker; 1993)
A charged account of Bill Clinton's 1992 presidential electoral campaign.

Best of Enemies
(Robert Gordon, Morgan Neville; 2015)
How Gore Vidal and William F. Buckley's 1968 on-air clashes transformed political coverage on US TV.

The Kingmaker
(Lauren Greenfield; 2019)
A portrait of Imelda Marcos and her attempts to return to political life in the Philippines.

MINAMATA: THE VICTIMS AND THEIR WORLD

MINAMATA: KANJA-SAN TO SONO SEKAI
NORIAKI TSUCHIMOTO; JAPAN; 1971; 167/120 MINS (INT'L VERSION)

ALSO SEE

The House is Black
(p.212)

Darwin's Nightmare
(Hubert Sauper; 2005)
The introduction of a breed of fish in Tanzania's Lake Victoria proves disastrous for the environment.

Gasland
(Josh Fox; 2010)
A portrait of communities in the US who claim to have been adversely affected by fracking.

Sennan Asbestos Disaster
(Kazuo Hara; 2016)
An account of the legal battle waged by citizens of the Sennan district of Osaka against the Japanese government, due to the proximity of asbestos factories.

Noriaki Tsuchimoto's powerful film details the devastating impact of mercury poisoning in a small coastal city on Kyūshū, the southernmost of Japan's four main islands. The filmmaker charts the rising tide of public protest, the ineffectiveness of government and the devastating consequences for a small fishing community.

Since its inception in 1932, the Nihon Chisso Fertilizer company emptied untreated mercury sulphate into local waters, which made its way into the ecosystem, contaminating water and food, and then animals and humans. The resulting neurological disease caused muscle weakness, loss of vision, hearing and speech, and in extreme cases insanity, coma and death. Human casualties were first reported in 1951, with the toll gradually increasing over the next few decades.

In 1965, Tsuchimoto made a short TV documentary about what was happening in the area. He returned in 1970, but this time he and his small crew lived within the affected community for four months. They detailed the profound impact of Chisso's negligence towards individuals who lost loved ones to the disease and families struggling to help living victims, alongside the social stigma the disease provoked within the community. Much of the film is taken up by Tsuchimoto's interviews with affected families – the pain of victims' relatives as difficult to watch as the deformities caused by the poisoning. The film also focuses on the actions of affected families and supporters, culminating in extraordinary scenes at a Chisso shareholders meeting in 1970, which features an emotional and embittered encounter between the mother of an affected child and the evasive head of the company.

Tsuchimoto saw what happened in Minamata as part of a wider malaise in contemporary Japan. As he noted around the time of the film's release: 'Minamata had been forgotten for 17 years. This abandonment, this silence, was perhaps a symptom of the power of capitalism, of non-caring authorities, of disengaged citizens.' He continued to make films about Minamata across his lifetime, most notably the lyrical, visually striking community portrait *The Shiranui Sea* (1975). And the cause of the Minamata population was subsequently taken up by Kazuo Hara who, over 15 years, pieced together his six-hour documentary *Minamata Mandala* (2020), highlighting the significance of what took place within Japanese society.

POLITICS IS INSEPARABLE FROM CINEMA . . .

Pere Portabella

EL SOPAR

PERE PORTABELLA;
SPAIN; 1974; 47 MINS

An experimental filmmaker known for his radicalism records a dinner conversation between five former political prisoners. What transpires is riveting – an intimate portrait from the front line of the fight for political freedom and human rights.

The dinner took place on 2 March 1974, the day that Catalan anarchist Salvador Puig Antich was executed. General Francisco Franco was still the head of Spain's military dictatorship and would be for another 18 months. His death on 20 November 1975 prompted the country's gradual move towards democracy. Neither the five former prisoners nor the crew shooting the film are named. (A version of the film released in 1976 would include them in its credits.) But as they prepare their meal, we are informed of each activist's role in opposing Franco's government and that their combined prison time totals 50 years.

The idyllic rural setting and the variety of sumptuous dishes served over the course of the evening contrasts markedly with the tone of the conversation. It opens with discussion of communes and their effectiveness in relation to the success of political action, but soon turns darker. The guests talk about their incarceration and the limited opportunities for activism available to political prisoners. Evincing a frankness that might have been less forthright on a public stage, the speakers debate the benefits of actions such as hunger strikes, agreeing that they will only work if a publicity machine succeeds in communicating them to the wider public. From there, the interaction becomes more intimate as each reflects on the psychological impact of their time in prison – the erosion of their identity and being. The weightiness is momentarily leavened by one member of the group, who recalls enjoying some moments of solitude in captivity, away from the constant demands of political action.

An iconic figure in Spanish cinema, Portabella's 50-year career is dominated by films with a combative edge, particularly those dealing with the Franco regime. *El Sopar* can be seen as a companion piece to his subsequent *General Report on Certain Matters of Interest for a Public Screening* (1977), made in the aftermath of Franco's death and documenting the emergence of a new political class and their fight for democracy, which the guests in *El Sopar* sacrificed so much for.

ALSO SEE

Waltz with Bashir
(p.146)

The Spanish Earth
(Joris Ivens; 1937)
An account of the Spanish Republican government's attempts to battle a rebellion by Franco's forces.

General Report on Certain Matters of Interest for a Public Screening
(Pere Portabella; 1976)
A record of an attempt to form a democracy in Spain following the death of Franco.

The Basque Ball: Skin Against Stone
(Julio Medem; 2003)
An exploration of the competing voices in the Spanish region's long campaign to achieve autonomy.

HARLAN COUNTY, USA

BARBARA KOPPLE;
US; 1976; 103 MINS

Barbara Kopple's Oscar-winning account of a violent miners' strike in Kentucky detailed decades of mistreatment by the mine's owners. It also highlighted the solidarity of the close-knit workers' community and the key role women – co-workers, mothers, wives and daughters – played in the campaign.

After serving in the John F. Kennedy-initiated Volunteers in Service to America (VISTA) programme, Kopple cut her teeth on documentaries, assisting Albert and David Maysles on their influential *Salesman* (1969) and *Gimme Shelter* (1970). The documentary she initially envisioned was to focus on the corrupt rule of United Mine Workers of America (UMWA) representative W.A. 'Tony' Boyle in the late 1960s. But as the 1973 strike at the Brookside Mine and Prep Plant in Harlan County attracted national headlines, she shifted her focus, recording the daily hardships faced by the miners in their fight for a decent wage, healthcare and fair industrial representation.

Deeply suspicious of any outside involvement, the miners and their families were initially uneasy about the crew's presence. Kopple only earned their trust by her willingness to remain at their side, even when tensions with the mine owners increased. The danger to the miners is palpable as they attempt to prevent workers crossing the picket line.

ALSO SEE

The Battle of Chile
(p.134)

Men and Dust
(Lee Dick; 1940)
An experimental short, profiling the hardships faced by a coalmining community in Oklahoma.

American Dream
(Barbara Kopple; 1990)
Kopple details the travails of striking workers at the Hormel meatpacking plant in Minnesota.

Still the Enemy Within
(Owen Gower; 2014)
An account of the 1984–85 British miners' strike, told by those on the front line.

THE COAL MINER WILL ALWAYS BE A FIGHTER

In one early morning encounter, featured in the film, Kopple and her camera operator Hart Perry were also attacked. The filmmaker later found out that this was an attempt on their lives, to ensure that no record would remain of what took place.

The filmmakers spent over 18 months in Harlan County. They captured countless conversations between the miners and their families, and encounters with company officials and the enforcers employed to keep the mine running during the strike. Kopple also sourced archive footage of the violent strikes that took place in the area in the 1930s. It highlights a history of oppressive corporate tactics, social and economic negligence and a total lack of concern for the wellbeing of the miners and their families. Featuring Hazel Dickens' impassioned folk songs, which chronicle the perennial struggle of the miners, and highlighting the activism of the miners' wives who were key to the strike's success, Kopple's film is an unvarnished portrait of a community who refuse to surrender to the bullying tactics of big business.

A GRIN WITHOUT A CAT

LE FOND DE L'AIR EST ROUGE
CHRIS MARKER; FRANCE;
1977/1993; 240/178 MINS

An exhaustive assemblage of archive footage, culled from news reports, propaganda and the work of collectivist groups, Chris Marker's expansive cine-essay looks back to the protests that took place in the late 1960s to assess why the revolutionary spirit of that era failed to bring about significant change.

The film opens with footage from Sergei Eisenstein's revolutionary classic *Battleship Potemkin* (1925), then shifts focus to post-revolutionary Cuba, the Vietnam War and social unrest around the world throughout the 1960s. An ambitious undertaking, dazzlingly realized and so inventive in its construction, it is impossible to conceive that it could have been made by anyone but the visionary Marker, who directed the landmark 1962 sci-fi short *La Jetée* and acclaimed 1983 travelogue *Sans Soleil*.

The excerpts from Eisenstein's film are juxtaposed against footage of various armed forces attempting to quell demonstrations. Marker had been at the forefront of the revolutionary cause in May 1968, but here the filmmaker identifies 1967 as the key year. The Cuban revolution gave a sense of hope and the escalation of the Vietnam War – and opposition to it – should have been the spark that ushered in change. But the film identifies more traditional forces on the left that had become institutionalized and saw the acquisition of power within the current system as its goal. The students of 1968 (the grin of the film's title) soon realized that the world they envisaged (the cat) was not a vision shared by everyone. Marker's film explores a compendium of events to show how the betrayal of revolutionary values began in the lead up to that tumultuous year and then unfurled around the world.

The film was originally released in a four-hour version. Marker recut the footage in 1993, reducing it by an hour and adding a coda that reflected on more recent events, concluding that capitalism 'won the battle, if not the war'. He gives himself an editing and soundtrack credit only, instead highlighting the importance of those who fight for their cause but are rarely recognized and without whom his challenging and overlooked film could not exist: 'The true authors of this film are the countless cameramen, technical operators, witnesses and activists whose work is constantly pitted against that of the powers that be, who would like us to have no memory.'

ROGER & ME

MICHAEL MOORE;
US; 1989; 91 MINS

Michael Moore's feature debut set the template for his polarizing mode of filmmaking. Combining investigative documentary, satirical montages and asides, and staged set-pieces, all infused with a sense of moral outrage, *Roger & Me* details the impact of corporate decision-making upon the citizens of Moore's home town of Flint, Michigan.

In the late 1980s, General Motors decided to significantly reduce its operations in Flint, relocating much of the work to Mexico and investing the money saved by the move in technology and munitions. The largest employer in the town, GM's decision, overseen by CEO Roger Smith, proved disastrous to the local economy. Generations of Moore's family had worked for the company and so he decided to document the impact of the redundancies on the community. Central to his film was gaining access to Smith himself, a manoeuvre later echoed in *Bowling for Columbine* (2002) and *Capitalism: A Love Story* (2009), where Moore attempted to confront the CEOs of Walmart and Goldman Sachs.

The filmmaker visits old school friends and other former employees, now struggling to survive, while documenting the work of a local sheriff's deputy charged with evicting tenants. He contrasts these lives with portraits of Flint's wealthy populace, many of whom are GM executives. The juxtaposition between these worlds is often as inspired as it is unsettling. In one sequence Moore follows some ex-GM workers, now prison guards, who find themselves processing former colleagues who turned to crime, while affluent members of Flint society are happy to pay $100 to party the night away in a recently constructed, soon-to-be-opened jail.

Critics have taken umbrage with Moore's manipulation of facts and events to prove his point – a position that intensified following the release of *Bowling for Columbine* and *Fahrenheit 9/11* (2004). But these criticisms miss the point of Moore's films; they are the work of an activist filmmaker who is damning of a culture that cares little for community and the lives that hold it together.

Roger & Me ends with ironic use of the Beach Boys' 'Wouldn't It Be Nice' and a warning: 'As we neared the end of the twentieth century, the rich were richer, the poor poorer... It was truly the dawn of a new era.' It's a thesis that Moore would continue to explore in subsequent films.

PROPAGANDA

For its first 60 years, cinema was the perfect platform for mass propaganda. Its universal appeal and emotional power, combined with rapid advances in technology, allowed for the manipulation of information and audiences.

J. Stuart Blackton and Albert E. Smith's *Tearing Down the Spanish Flag* (1898), a popular single-shot film referencing the Spanish-American War, was one of the earliest examples. D.W. Griffith's racist *The Birth of a Nation* (1915) advanced the sophistication of propaganda in narrative cinema. But it wasn't until the work of Soviet Constructivist and Nazi filmmakers in the 1920s and 1930s that documentary hit its stride.

Soviet Constructivist films like *Man with a Movie Camera* (1929, p.16) employed radical editing techniques to form a commentary on society through the assembly of often disparate images. While in Germany, Leni Riefenstahl's *Triumph of the Will* (1935), a record of the sixth Nazi Party Congress in 1934, reflected Hitler's desire for a monumental cinema style to represent his vision of the Third Reich. And films like Fritz Hippler's

The Eternal Jew (1940) brandished the Nazis' anti-Semitic ideology. The countries opposing the Nazis ramped up their propaganda machines as war approached, eventually producing effective films from the war and home front. Films like *London Can Take It!* (1940) and *Listen to Britain* (1942) proved hugely effective, as did Frank Capra's expansive *Why We Fight* series (1942–45). The effectiveness of these films was highlighted in the series *The World at War* (1973–74, p.133).

Increasing public ambivalence to conflicts and the fracturing of societies across cultural, moral and political divides since the early 1960s, evinced by films like *A Grin Without a Cat* (1977/1993, p.64) and *Hearts and Minds* (1974, p.136), witnessed a rising opposition to overt state propaganda. Television, online advertising and the rise of social media would eventually prove more successful in their interaction with everyday life. But the language and style of propaganda film remains influential. And the work of environmental activists, anti-war campaigners and conspiracy theorists shows that propaganda in the twenty-first century is no longer solely the remit of those in power.

Opposite: Leni Riefenstahl shooting
Triumph of the Will (1935)
Right: *Why We Fight* (1942–45)

HOOP DREAMS

STEVE JAMES;
US; 1994; 170 MINS

ALSO SEE

Rize
(p.112)

The Heart of the Game
(Ward Serrill; 2005)
Charting the highs and lows of a
Seattle high school girls' basketball
team over six seasons.

The Australian Dream
(Daniel Gordon; 2019)
Racist abuse aimed at Australian
rules footballer Adam Goodes is
the starting point for an exploration
of race and identity.

The Last Dance
(Jason Hehir; 2020)
A detailed and expansive hagiography
of legendary basketball star
Michael Jordan.

Steve James' intimate epic is one of the defining sports documentaries, a moving human drama and an unflinching portrait of the economic and social divide in the US. It details the challenges facing African American teens as they attempt to realize their dream of playing professional basketball in the NBA, whose natural talent and ambition is eclipsed by the severity of their circumstances.

William Gates and Arthur Agee hail from Cabrini-Green and West Garfield Park, two of Chicago's more economically impoverished neighbourhoods. Basketball is their lifeblood. Their parents support them as much as they can, but opportunities are limited. However, hope arrives in the form of sports scholarships to a prestigious Catholic prep school in Westchester, Illinois. But the challenge of a 90-minute commute, balancing academic studies with a rigorous physical regimen and a social climate that is completely alien to them gradually takes its toll.

James' film was originally intended to be a 30-minute documentary for PBS. But the filmmaker's interest in his subjects, and the realization that their story reflected wider issues facing African American communities, broadened the film's scope, transforming it into a five-year shoot. Charting the boys' journey from age 14 to 19, starting in their eighth grade and ending in the first year of college, James and co-editors Frederick Marx and Peter Gilbert whittled down 250 hours into a compelling narrative. (It remains the only documentary to receive an Academy Award nomination for editing.)

James makes clear that the social and economic problems the boys face are their biggest obstacles. He captures them rising before their families each weekday morning, as they confront the bluster of a Chicago winter to make their way to school, then having to perform to the limit of their abilities in the classroom and on the court, before making the same arduous journey home each night and completing whatever homework has been set. They are also forced to confront various domestic problems. But when James captures them on court, in training and during games, they become transformed. It's in these moments that *Hoop Dreams* excels, when William and Arthur can almost touch the life they ultimately realize they will never have.

I SET OUT TO DO A FILM ABOUT WHAT BASKETBALL MEANS

Steve James

TO YOUNG PEOPLE LIKE ARTHUR AND WILLIAM.

IF YOU THINK THE WORLD WAS SURPRISED WHEN NIXON RESIGNED,

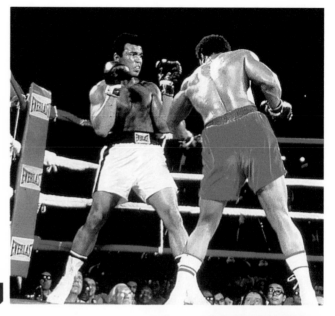

WAIT TILL I KICK FOREMAN'S BEHIND.

Muhammad Ali

WHEN WE WERE KINGS

LEON GAST; US;
1996; 88 MINS

The 1974 world heavyweight championship match between former titleholder Muhammad Ali and reigning champion George Foreman was less a boxing match than a global cultural event. Leon Gast's sprightly-paced account draws on a rich trove of archive footage to detail events as they unfolded. The film also locates the fight – along with the hoopla that surrounded it – within the wider arena of culture and politics.

Frequently cited by pundits as the greatest sporting event of the twentieth century and dubbed by Ali the 'Rumble in the Jungle', the match took place on 30 October in Kinshasa, the capital of Zaire (now the Democratic Republic of the Congo). More than 60,000 people were in attendance for the fight and there was an estimated television audience of one billion, making it the most-watched live television broadcast at that time. It was the brainchild of promoter Don King, a charismatic character with a penchant for quoting Shakespeare, whose reputation was cemented by the event's success. He promised each fighter five million dollars, an amount that Zaire's president Mobutu Sese Seko was happy to hand over in return for the tsunami of publicity that the event would attract.

When We Were Kings captures the intensity of Ali and Foreman's rivalry as they train and promote the event. It intercuts film of the music festival that took place in September, just before the original date of the fight, which had to be postponed by six weeks after Foreman received a cut above his eye during training. And it includes commentary by writers Norman Mailer and George Plimpton, who were present at the fight and talk of it as though it was a battle to the death. Gast's film also acknowledges the political climate in Zaire at the time and Mobutu's historical use of the stadium where the fight took place to torture thousands of political opponents.

Events leading up to the fight prove so dramatic and compelling – as was Ali, a natural performer in and out of the ring – that the match itself doesn't begin until an hour into the film. Gast successfully recreates the suspense that made it such a sporting landmark. He also conveys the sense of shock and jubilation at Ali's unorthodox rope-a-dope tactics, which enabled him to defeat the towering Foreman and establish him as one of the sporting world's greatest icons.

WEST OF THE TRACKS

TIE XI QU
WANG BING; CHINA/
NETHERLANDS; 2002; 551 MINS

Divided into three parts and spanning nine hours, Wang Bing's documentary details the gradual decline of industry in Tiexi District, in the northwest Chinese city of Shenyang. Filmed between 1999 and 2001, *West of the Tracks* captures a moment when the country's socialist economy was being replaced by free market opportunism, at the expense of a vast army of workers and the social amenities that supported them. It is a landmark of observational documentary by a dissident filmmaker who immerses himself fully in the worlds of his subjects.

Tiexi was originally built to produce armaments for the Japanese Imperial Army in the 1930s. With Mao Zedong's rise to power it became the base of heavy industry, with materials supplied by the Soviet Union for the brief period that the two countries' worldview was aligned. In the 1970s and 1980s, following the Cultural Revolution, there was a surge in employment that rejuvenated the region. But as a new China emerged in the 1990s, Tiexi found itself left behind. When *West of the Tracks* begins, factories face bankruptcy and closure, residential neighbourhoods are being demolished and a large work population faces displacement.

The film opens with a shot from the front of a train as it journeys through Tiexi's vast, increasingly dilapidated industrial infrastructure. The first part, 'Rust', focuses on what manual work there is, interspersing moments of activity with conversations between the temporary employees. It ends with news of various factories' imminent closure. 'Remnants' is set among the inhabitants of 'Rainbow Row', the name of a prominent working-class neighbourhood. It charts the residents' attempts to cope with the changes and the lack of opportunities available to them. 'Rails' focuses on the transport artery that runs through the region. As the factories shut, the demand for trains to and from Tiexi lessens, placing another workforce in limbo.

Employing long takes and extended tracking shots, Wang Bing balances the scale of social upheaval in the region – a vast city being forcibly shuttered – with frank and unsentimental portraits of a population that progress has left behind. An ambitious debut by the filmmaker, it set the tone for his subsequent work, which has been equally critical of his country's embrace of 'progress' and the price paid by the millions who struggle to keep up.

IF YOU SHOW
SOMEBODY'S LIFE

OVER A LONG PERIOD

THEN YOU COME TO UNDERSTAND
HIM OR HER BETTER.

Wang Bing

NOSTALGIA FOR THE LIGHT

PATRICIO GUZMÁN; FRANCE/
GERMANY/CHILE/SPAIN; 2010;
90 MINS

Science, politics, history and the natural world intersect as Patricio Guzmán links his country's landscape with its past. Whereas his earlier *The Battle of Chile* (1975–79, p.134) was a startling revolutionary work that captured the fervour of a turbulent era, *Nostalgia for the Light* is a more philosophical rumination on the history of a people and their environment.

The filmmaker had hopes of becoming an astronomer when he was young. He regularly visited an observatory in Santiago, a city that 'slept in the foothills of the Cordillera, detached from the rest of the world'. But his dreams were interrupted by a popular revolution that 'swept us to the centre of the world' and a coup d'état that installed the brutal military dictatorship of General Augusto Pinochet. In his film, Guzmán regards the Atacama Desert as the physical embodiment of the juncture between science and politics. One of the driest places on Earth, its altitude and atmosphere make it the perfect location to study the heavens, with networks of observatories and radio telescopes populating the landscape. But beneath its surface is evidence of extinguished lives: victims of Pinochet's rule are buried across the terrain. As astronomers gaze upwards, the relatives of those who were disappeared scour for remains. One mother ponders the idea of the powerful telescopes pointing downwards to 'see through the earth so that we could find them'.

Guzmán draws further parallels between celestial and more Earth-bound bodies. A camera appears to pan over the surface of the moon only to pull away and reveal the roof of a skull. A desert shrouded in mist turns out to be preserved body parts protected by tissue. And there is an emotional connection between recent history and science, when one young astronomer whose parents were killed during Pinochet's regime notes, 'I am convinced that memory has a gravitational force'.

Like Guzmán's subsequent *The Pearl Button* (2015) and *The Cordillera of Dreams* (2019), featuring striking imagery that underpins much of the filmmaker's later work, *Nostalgia for the Light* skilfully juxtaposes Chile's political and social history against the ebb and flow of the natural world. Here, revolutionary fervour has been replaced by reflection, over what has been lost and what remains to be discovered, both beneath the ground and in the universe above our heads.

ALSO SEE

The Battle of Chile
(p.134)

Salvatore Allende
(Patricio Guzman; 2004)
A portrait of the murdered
Chilean president.

The City of Photographers
(Sebastián Moreno; 2006)
A record of the role played by
photographers in documenting life
under the Pinochet regime.

Coup 53
(Taghi Amirani; 2019)
An account of the coup that
overthrew Iranian prime minister
Mohammad Mosaddegh in 1953.

I THINK THAT LIFE IS MEMORY.

EVERYTHING IS MEMORY.

Patricio Guzmán

THE QUEEN OF VERSAILLES

LAUREN GREENFIELD; US/
NETHERLANDS/UK/DENMARK;
2012; 100 MINS

Lauren Greenfield's feature debut began as a portrait of timeshare property tycoon David Siegel's family during construction of the largest private home in the US. But the fallout of the 2008 economic crisis transformed the film into a surreal barometer of the times.

A photographer whose work has focused on consumerism and the accumulation of wealth, Greenfield first met Jackie Siegel on a shoot with Donatella Versace. One of the designer's best customers, Jackie surprised Greenfield with her openness – a trait the photographer rarely found in the wealthy. Upon hearing about the house Jackie and David were building in Florida, equally inspired by the eponymous French palace and the Paris Hotel in Las Vegas, she convinced them to let her film their daily life.

Opening with a photo shoot, *The Queen of Versailles* initially profiles the Siegels' world, one untroubled by economic constraints but burdened by the excesses of uninhibited affluence. It then shifts to the impact of the 2008 crash on the family and how their lives change as a result. Or, as David disingenuously describes it, 'this is a riches to rags story'. As with her subsequent feature documentary *The Kingmaker* (2019), detailing Imelda Marcos' return to the Philippines and her family's gradually re-emergence on the political scene, Greenfield's filmmaking style gives her subjects the space to reveal themselves. And the filmmaker knows how to frame their world, from the gaudiness of individual and family portraits to their unceasing need to spend.

A snapshot of Western culture in the twenty-first century, *The Queen of Versailles* is fascinating, frequently funny, but ultimately unsettling. It is more contained than other documentaries that tackle the fallout of the 2008 economic crisis and the growing chasm between rich and poor. But Greenfield understands what the Siegels represent. At one point David claims: 'Everyone wants to be rich. If they can't be rich the next best thing is to feel rich.' The timeshare company he owns purports to feed that desire, as well as funding his family's excesses. David's estimation of his own importance may grate – he claims to have been crucial in George W. Bush's 2000 election victory – but to many he and Jackie achieved the American Dream. Greenfield's film begs us to consider what that dream now represents and whether it is in the collective interest of all who aspire to it.

ALSO SEE

Roger & Me
(p.65)

Capitalism: A Love Story
(Michael Moore; 2009)
Moore takes a critical journey around the US in the wake of the country's economic collapse.

Road to Las Vegas
(Jason Massot; 2010)
A family hoping to improve their lot by moving to the construction mecca of Las Vegas soon find their dreams souring.

Generation Wealth
(Lauren Greenfield; 2018)
A decade-long, multi-platform project exploring consumer culture around the world.

HOW TO SURVIVE A PLAGUE

DAVID FRANCE; US; 2012;
110 MINS

This moving history of ACT UP (AIDS Coalition to Unleash Power) draws its strength from a compelling assembly of archive news and home movie footage, alongside passionate testimonies by activists on the front line of the campaign in the 1980s and 1990s. Charting the rise of HIV (human immunodeficiency virus) in the US – and New York in particular – David France's film is a powerful tribute to an organization and the individuals in it whose work saved the lives of thousands.

In 1987, the worldwide death toll from AIDS was 500,000. By 1995, when combination therapy was found to be the key to successfully treating the virus, over eight million had lost their lives. ACT UP was created in 1987 by a group of activists who despaired at the apathy of the medical establishment and the lack of activity by New York Mayor Ed Koch in response to the crisis. They fought for the rights of those who had succumbed to the virus and for a way to treat it.

Sourced from more than 700 hours of footage, France's film opens in the early days of the epidemic, which saw New York hospitals turning away patients and an escalation of homophobic violence on the city's streets. He was an integral part of the movement and his proximity to key individuals is invaluable to the film – his interviews with survivors highlight how the years of tireless campaigning led to seismic change. It also makes him a judicious director of archive footage. He not only draws together significant moments from the era, but highlights the work of key individuals, from playwright Larry Kramer, PR executive-turned-activist Bob Rafsky and former bond trader Peter Staley to film archivist Mark Harrington, whose skill at reading medical reports saw him join the Treatment Action Group, which would make extraordinary strides in pushing research in the right direction.

How to Survive a Plague is exhaustive in its recounting of the works of a dedicated and passionate group, and the sacrifices they made. It acknowledges the pain and loss that was felt by so many. But France ultimately presents what happened as an extraordinary victory for a group that had little money, faced a seemingly insurmountable opposition and were racing against time.

ALSO SEE

Paris is Burning
(p.37)

*Common Threads:
Stories from the Quilt*
(Rob Epstein, Jeffrey Friedman; 1989)
The story of the NAMES Project AIDS Memorial Quilt, dedicated to those who died of AIDS-related causes.

Vito
(Jeffrey Schwartz; 2011)
A portrait of the AIDS activist and author of *The Celluloid Closet*, Vito Russo.

Fire in the Blood
(Dylan Mohan Gray; 2013)
How a coalition fought against pharmaceutical giants to supply AIDS drugs to developing countries.

I WANT FUTURE GENERATIONS TO KNOW THE PROFOUND CONTRIBUTIONS TO AMERICAN LIFE – AND GLOBAL HEALTH CARE

THAT IS THE LEGACY OF AIDS ACTIVISM.

CITIZENFOUR

LAURA POITRAS;
US/GERMANY/UK; 2014;
114 MINS

ALSO SEE

The Power of Nightmares
(p.142)

*The Most Dangerous Man in
America: Daniel Ellsberg and
the Pentagon Papers*
(Judith Ehrlich, Rick Goldsmith; 2009)
An account of the first major
political whistleblower in the US.

1971
(Johanna Hamilton; 2014)
The story of a break-in at an FBI
office that exposed the widespread
wiretapping of US citizens.

The Great Hack
(Karim Amer, Jehane Noujaim; 2019)
The Cambridge Analytica scandal is
the launching point for a chilling
overview of political manipulation.

Laura Poitras' film is an urgent, as-it-happened account of the moment US security employee Edward Snowden became one of the world's most famous whistle-blowers. On 6 June 2013, British newspaper the *Guardian* published the first in a series of reports by journalist Glenn Greenwald that detailed the US government's mass surveillance of its own citizens. Four days later, Snowden voluntarily revealed himself to be the source of the controversial revelations. Poitras was with him as he talked to Greenwald and her film increases in tension as it details the frantic days around the publication of the documents, offering a portrait of an individual who, with nothing to gain, felt an obligation to highlight the erosion of US citizens' rights.

As Poitras notes at the beginning of her film, she was already a 'person of interest' for US authorities, having previously made the documentary *My Country, My Country* (2006), which was critical of US involvement in Iraq. In *Citizenfour*'s first section, Poitras recounts her earliest conversations, via encrypted messages, with her eponymous contact, interspersing the communications with details regarding the burgeoning surveillance sector in the US and the refutation by officials that there was any mass surveillance of the US populace. The film then shifts to a hotel in Hong Kong where Poitras, Greenwald and *Guardian* journalist Ewan MacAskill meet with Snowden and discuss the vast trove of data he is handing over, which reveals 'a system whose reach is unlimited but whose safeguards are not'. From the outset, Snowden shows little regard for his own wellbeing, accepting the repercussions of his actions, but making clear no one else was involved in the decision. He also stresses the importance of not publishing any information that could harm individuals working in either the military or security forces.

Playing out in real-time, with the record of Snowden's attempts to evade capture resembling a political thriller, *Citizenfour* lucidly details the complexity of inter-government surveillance of everyday life. It ends with the US government initiating its attempt to bring Snowden to task for his 'crime', suggesting his actions are more detrimental to society than the information he revealed. But Snowden makes clear his actions were prompted by a belief in the rule of law and that everyone, including governments, are subservient to it.

13TH

AVA DUVERNAY;
US; 2016; 100 MINS

The 13th Amendment to the United States Constitution was intended to abolish slavery and involuntary servitude. But the inclusion of the clause 'except as a punishment for crime whereof the party shall have been duly convicted' saw imprisonment weaponized, particularly against the country's Black population. It became a new form of slavery. Ava DuVernay's comprehensive history of how the amendment has been manipulated by politicians, law enforcement agencies and corporations, journeys from the post-Civil War Reconstruction era through to the present, arguing that prejudice and bigotry has remained a constant in US life.

Employing a rich trove of archive material (newspaper illustrations, photographs and film footage), making effective – but sparing – use of animation, and featuring interviews with academics, lawyers, writers and politicians, *13th* details how American society has accepted myths as facts over the course of the last 150 years. It begins with the demonization of the 'menacing negro male' that made mass incarceration of African Americans in the late nineteenth century more palatable, followed by the rise of white supremacy – particularly after the success of D.W. Griffith's racist tract *The Birth of a Nation* (1915) – and the introduction of the segregationist Jim Crow laws. The film then progresses, at a brisk pace, through to the present day. It tackles the militarization of police forces around the country and the deployment of loaded phrases such as 'wolf pack' and 'super-predators', which promulgated the same old myths and helped usher in draconian policies and laws that prolonged prison time. Politicians' claims of bringing in changes for the good of society are summarily dismissed by some speakers, including former political activist Angela Davis, who notes: 'Historically, when one looks at efforts to create reform they inevitably lead to more repression.'

DuVernay also looks at the role of corporate America, whose vested interest in the business of prisons saw them actively promoting prolonged incarceration, and more recently successfully monetizing the parole system. Ending with a focus on the series of police shootings that saw the emergence of the Black Lives Matter movement, *13th* is a powerful and essential journey through a century of prejudice that ends with the suggestion that the US teeters on a precipice, and that its course can only be altered through a radical change in perspective. As poet and activist Malkia Cyril concludes, 'It's about changing the way this country understands human dignity.'

FIRE AT SEA

FUOCOAMMARE
GIANFRANCO ROSI; ITALY/
FRANCE; 2016; 108 MINS

Gianfranco Rosi's film looks at the European migrant crisis through the prism of life on a small island that lies between the southernmost point of Italy and the North African coastline. One of the most striking documentaries to grapple with this issue, it's an essential portrait of the local inhabitants and the thousands that arrive by boat, seeking refuge.

The island of Lampedusa covers eight square miles. It lies 120 miles from Sicily and 70 miles from Tunisia. It has a population of 6,000, whose main industries are fishing, farming and tourism. In the first half of the 2010s, more than 400,000 migrants landed on the island, while approximately 15,000 died at sea, making it the deadliest migrant route in the world.

Fire at Sea balances portraits of the islanders with footage shot aboard Navy vessels and the migrants' boats. Their lives are, for the most part, seen in exclusion from each other, with Rosi highlighting the gulf that exists between the two. There is Samuele Pucillo, a young boy with sight problems, his grandmother, a radio DJ, some of his elderly listeners, a diver and a fisherman. One of Lampedusa's doctors treats the local populace and the new arrivals. He states, 'It is the duty of every human being, if you're human, to help these people'. The film focuses on a variety of refugees in order to highlight the scale of the crisis. But Rosi is careful not to treat them solely in terms of numbers, robbing them of their identities. A woman appears inconsolable over what she has lost during her journey. A group of men sing of their experiences, as another exclaims: 'The mountains could not hide us. The people could not hide us ... we run to the sea.'

Like Rosi's earlier *Sacro GRA* (2013) and subsequent *Notturno* (2020), *Fire at Sea* is strikingly beautiful. The imagery doesn't negate the film of its power to shock. But it does afford Rosi's subjects – from the migrants and locals alike, to those working to help them – a dignity that is sometimes missing from films tackling this issue.

IN THE END, THE FILM IS A CRY FOR HELP.

Gianfranco Rosi

I AM NOT YOUR NEGRO

RAOUL PECK; SWITZERLAND/
FRANCE/BELGIUM/US/GERMANY/
UK; 2016; 93 MINS

ALSO SEE

13th
(p.81)

Strange Victory
(Leo Hurwitz; 1948)
A chronicle of Black American GIs returning
home from the Second World War, only
to face prejudice and persecution.

Take This Hammer
(Richard O. Moore; 1964)
James Baldwin's journey around
San Francisco highlights the
prevalence of racial segregation.

Nat Turner: A Troublesome Property
(Charles Burnett; 2003)
A critical examination of the life, actions
and legacy of Nat Turner and how
his story has been represented.

Raoul Peck's documentary is a chronicle of racism in the US, viewed through the prism of the life, work and letters of James Baldwin. One of the most gifted writers of his generation, whose landmark works include *Go Tell It on the Mountain* and *Another Country,* from the late 1950s Baldwin became a passionate advocate for civil rights. In the summer of 1957, he returned to the US from self-imposed exile in Paris. He had left his country because of the racism he experienced, yet it was images of that same bigotry that brought him back. He threw himself into the Civil Rights Movement and through his eloquence, intelligence and wit became a prominent spokesperson for the Black cause. In doing so, he befriended NAACP organizer Medgar Evers, Malcolm X and Martin Luther King Jr. Their assassinations, between 1963 and 1969, engulfed him in grief, but also enraged him. *I Am Not Your Negro* traces Baldwin's attempt to articulate what these important figures meant to him.

Divided into chapters and with Baldwin's words spoken by Samuel L. Jackson, *I Am Not Your Negro* makes stunning use of archive footage to detail a country divided. It opens by contextualizing life for Black Americans that followed the Second World War; a country that 'has not in its whole system of reality evolved any place for you'. Peck presents Baldwin's examination of how discriminatory white representations of African Americans dominated popular culture, illustrating his argument with a variety of films and TV programmes, from musicals to Westerns.

The film not only documents the escalating violence towards the Black populace across the US, it also details social and cultural restrictions that made life difficult for Black people. Finally, Peck draws together Baldwin's thoughts on the future and how the decades since the writer's death have witnessed continued infringements upon African Americans' safety and liberty. These themes echo Baldwin's pained response to the murder of his friends and his hopes for the country's future. It ends with Baldwin stating, 'I am not a pessimist, because I'm alive'. But for the US to survive, Baldwin notes, it must reconcile itself with its past.

MAIDEN

ALEX HOLMES;
UK; 2018; 97 MINS

In 1989, the first all-female team entered the Whitbread Round the World Race. One of the most physically demanding and dangerous sporting events, 23 yachts of varying sizes spent an average of four-and-a-half months racing across six legs and a total distance of 32,018 miles. *Maiden*, one of the smallest vessels competing and skippered by Tracy Edwards, should have symbolized a landmark achievement. Instead, alongside the gruelling psychological and physical challenges of the race, the team had to overcome a barrage of sexism and misogyny. Alex Holmes' film is a celebratory account of the team's trials and success.

Interspersed with commentary by Edwards, former crew members, participants in the event and members of the media who covered the race, the film seamlessly combines archive television and home movie footage. Holmes briefly charts Edwards' youth, the rebellious streak that emerged following the death of her father and her growing interest in sailing, which included being a cook aboard one of the competing yachts in the 1985–86 race. It details her attempts to attract a sponsor and the transformation of the 58-foot *Maiden* into a sea-worthy racing vessel. It's made clear that Edwards' drive and her desire to win at all costs didn't sit easily with everyone, particularly some members of her team. But with the race approaching, this steely determination is what pushed the crew and their yacht past the starting line.

The ingrained sexism of the media's response – from both male and female commentators – is made clear soon after the all-female team is announced. But the most egregious voices were silenced by *Maiden*'s performance. After a shaky start, the yacht came first in its division after two arduous stages. Although a technical mishap resulted in their completing the race in second place, their return to the UK saw them hailed as heroes.

Holmes and editor Katie Bryer cut the film like a thrill-ride. Talking heads flesh out the interaction between key individuals and add colour to what took place, but never at the expense of pace. However, it's in the sequences filmed aboard the yacht, as the team push themselves to win and prove their detractors wrong, that the film excels. The result is an inspiring account of grit, determination and character in the face of challenging odds and petty prejudices.

ALSO SEE

Crip Camp
(p.90)

Maso and Miso Go Boating
(Nadja Ringart, Carole Roussopoulos, Delphine Seyrig, Ioana Wieder; 1975)
A TV broadcast is wilfully and wittily deconstructed to highlight misogyny in 1970s France.

Deep Water
(Louise Osmond, Jerry Rothwell; 2006)
The story of Donald Crowhurst's entry into a 1968 around the world solo yacht race and subsequent disappearance.

Freedom Fields
(Naziha Arebi; 2019)
An account of Libya's first female football team and the opposition they face.

INFINITE FOOTBALL

FOTBAL INFINIT
CORNELIU PORUMBOIU;
ROMANIA; 2018; 70 MINS

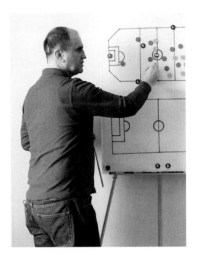

Corneliu Porumboiu's wry, low-key portrait of his old schoolfriend, a mid-level government administrator, is a disarming wonder. Laurentiu Ginghina has thought long and hard about football and decided it needs to change. Not in any superficial way, but a reinvention that would alter the mechanics of the beautiful game. And as the filmmaker presses his subject, Ginghina suggests that his ideas could be adopted as an ideology for living.

When he was nine, Ginghina sustained an injury during a schoolyard match. A sharp kick to the leg resulted in a fractured fibula. A year later, while working in a factory, he snapped his tibia. It happened as a result of the calcification of bones in the leg because of the first break. During a long walk home, he began to consider what happened in that game. He didn't blame the player who tackled him: 'It was the fault of imposed rules, norms, which weren't the best.' Over the years, he devised an alternative version of football. It would be played on an octagonal-shaped pitch to avoid the problem of corners, and players would be divided into various sectors. 'The ball has to be free,' Ginghina notes. And, as far as he is concerned, in the game's current iteration that isn't the case.

One of the key filmmakers of New Romanian Cinema, a loose collective that mostly came of age in the aftermath of Nicolae Ceauşescu's regime, Porumboiu has proven himself a sharp satirist whose minimalist aesthetic works well here. Ginghina could have been an easy target for the filmmaker. Instead, Porumboiu allows his friend to explore his ideas, filming him at the site of the childhood accident, his work (including a lovely moment when Ginghina generously tries to help an elderly visitor locate her property deeds), a football training session that employs his ideas and his childhood home. Ginghina reflects philosophically on missed chances and compares his working in an office while attempting to rewrite the rules of the world's most popular sport to a superhero's dual existence.

As Ginghina moves from football to promoting a more egalitarian society, in which his rules for a balanced game could be reflected in the structures of government and the way we interact, Porumboiu revels in his friend's vision. It's an affectionate portrait of an idealist who believes he can improve the game and, beyond that, the world.

I WAS VERY ATTRACTED TO THE STORY OF
THE RELATIONSHIP BETWEEN HISTORY, LAURENTIU'S DESTINY, AND

THE SPORT HE INVENTED.

FOR THE FIRST TIME, I REALLY FELT LIKE I HAD FREEDOM.

CRIP CAMP

JAMES LEBRECHT,
NICOLE NEWNHAM;
US; 2020; 106 MINS

Executive produced by Michelle and Barack Obama, this stirring, funny and occasionally provocative account of a summer camp for young adults living with various disabilities transforms into a fascinating record of a grassroots movement for social change. The film's genesis lies in a conversation between director Nicole Newnham and sound designer James Lebrecht, in which he described a seismic experience from his youth. Their collaboration celebrates a little-known story that challenges lazy stereotypes.

Located in the Catskill Mountains, in New York state, Camp Jened was established in 1951 as a variation on the traditional summer camp, catering to disabled children, teenagers and young adults. By the mid-1960s, it had embraced the countercultural scene and was regarded by attendees as a carefree utopia with little official supervision. LeBrecht, who was born with spina bifida, opens the film, discussing the way the camp freed him of his inhibitions and allowed him to pursue a successful career. *Crip Camp* then focuses on the summers of 1971–73 when a film crew from the People's Video Theater arrived to record daily life. The film makes rich use of what they witnessed, alongside present-day interviews with attendees. LeBrecht and Newnham's trump card in detailing events is not to shy away from any aspect of life at the camp. What might initially seem shocking – just as the film's name might arouse some consternation – is what makes *Crip Camp* so compelling. There is humour and frankness in the discussion of various challenges, from carrying out simple tasks to engaging in sex. Then the film shifts gear, to document how the freedom the attendees enjoyed at the camp influenced their decision to protest the way they were treated by society at large.

Through the work of many of Camp Jened's attendees, particularly celebrated campaigner Judith Heumann, Disabled in Action of Metropolitan New York (DIA) was formed in 1970. It would push for greater rights and access for the disabled population in the US. Years of campaigning finally led to the landmark Americans with Disabilities Act of 1990 and subsequent changes in governmental and corporate behaviour. Shining a light on this previously undocumented social history, *Crip Camp* successfully balances personal stories with the rise of a movement that brought about – and continues to fight for – much-needed change.

ALSO SEE

How to Survive a Plague
(p.78)

Sick: The Life and Death of Bob Flanagan, Supermasochist
(Kirby Dick; 1997)
A scabrously funny and ultimately moving portrait of the final years of the performance artist.

How's Your News?
(Arthur Bradford; 1999)
A group of aspiring journalists with varying disabilities travel the US to carry out on-the-street reports.

The Reason I Jump
(Jerry Rothwell; 2020)
Naoki Higashida's memoir provides the source material for a portrait of five non-speaking autistic youths.

ART &

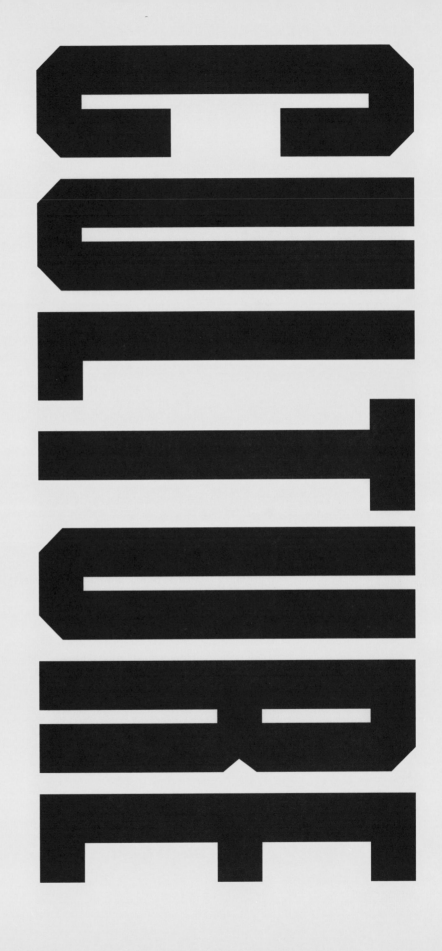

DON'T LOOK BACK

D.A. PENNEBAKER; US; 1967;
96 MINS

In 1965, Bob Dylan radically transformed his sound, shifting from a traditional folk outfit to an electric band. Three months earlier, D.A. Pennebaker filmed him as the focus of his feature directorial debut – an account of the iconic singer–songwriter's 11-day, 8-gig tour of England. The passage of time and changing fads in filmmaking have failed to eclipse the originality, energy and ebullience of Pennebaker's film, or the charisma of his occasionally truculent and perennially mercurial subject.

Don't Look Back is a stark contrast to the larky escapades of films from the mid-1960s that promoted bands like The Beatles (*A Hard Day's Night*, 1964; *Help!*, 1965) and The Monkees (from their TV series which began in 1966 to the surreal 1968 feature vehicle *Head*). Pennebaker's film pushed the aesthetics of direct cinema to the extreme. Save for the opening, a performance to camera of 'Subterranean Homesick Blues' that became the song's unofficial music video, Pennebaker's film comprises footage of Dylan backstage, between venues and in his hotel rooms, along with excerpts from his eight concerts.

For someone who became notoriously publicity-shy, Dylan is mostly relaxed on camera, an effect achieved by Pennebaker being a constant presence at the singer-songwriter's side. It also enabled the director to film others at work, including Dylan's wily manager and publicity agent, his friend Bob Neuwirth and the singer Alan Price. There are moments of tension with Joan Baez and both are captured in the process of writing songs. Dylan's ego emerges when he and Donovan share songs in a hotel room, and he erupts with rage when a party prank goes awry. He is provocative and playful with journalists, but deadly serious when it comes to his music.

Pennebaker shot on the hoof with light, portable equipment, occasionally in extremely low light. Almost invisible, he perfected his desire to be an unacknowledged presence in an environment. As he noted: 'We weren't the centre of the process; we were hardly visible. You wanted it to be real life; you didn't want to betray the process. If you didn't get something, you didn't get it.' What he did get cemented Dylan's iconic, pre-electric persona.

I ALWAYS THOUGHT OF MUSICIANS AS BEING THE SAINTS OF OUR TIME.

THEY LIVE FOR MUSIC, AND NOTHING ELSE IS INTERESTING TO THEM.

F FOR FAKE

ORSON WELLES; FRANCE/IRAN/
WEST GERMANY; 1973; 89 MINS

ALSO SEE

Exit Through the Gift Shop
(p.118)

A Man Vanishes
(Shōhei Imamura; 1967)
A film crew's search for a missing man
calls into question the relationship
between documentary and fiction.

This is Not a Film
(Jafar Panahi,
Mojtaba Mirtahmasb; 2011)
Under house arrest and banned from
filmmaking, Iranian filmmaker Panahi
reflects on the nature of his life and art.

Kate Plays Christine
(Robert Greene; 2016)
Actor Kate Lyn Sheil negotiates playing
Christine Chubbock, a TV journalist
who killed herself on air in 1974.

F for Fake questions the notion of authorship in film, writing and art. Neither a straightforward documentary nor narrative feature, filmmaker, actor, illusionist and raconteur Orson Welles' witty and playful cinematic essay explores the value of art and artistic enterprise, questions the veracity of truth and, in the film's later stages, successfully pulls off its own sleight-of-hand.

Welles' own past merges with his subjects' as he weaves his way in and out of the world of forgers, fraudsters and illusionists, both on the screen and in real life. His principal subjects are the art forger Elmyr de Hory and Clifford Irving, Elmyr's biographer and himself a forger, of the 'autobiography' of eccentric recluse Howard Hughes. Much of the de Hory and Irving footage is taken from a television documentary by François Reichenbach, who also appears here, but Welles integrates it into his film seamlessly. Elsewhere, he employs a trove of library footage and film excerpts, most notably when he recounts his 1938 *The War of the Worlds* radio dramatization, that caused panic among American listeners. It's not the only time Welles employed fakery as part of a greater project. His feature debut *Citizen Kane* (1941) open with an impressive pastiche of newsreel footage, which is also parodied in this film.

With its false starts, playing with the conventions of documentary and generous portraits of his subjects, *F for Fake* ponders modern society's fixation with authenticity; clearly an issue that pained him, following *The New Yorker* critic Pauline Kael's controversial 1971 essay 'Raising Kane', which questioned the extent of Welles' input into the creation of his acclaimed fictional biopic about a ruthlessly ambitious media mogul and political aspirant. But *F for Fake* is no sour rejoinder. It is a joyful celebration of illusion – in cinema, art and life – and the mavericks who revel in it. And as his film progresses, Welles draws his unwitting audience into his world of smoke and mirrors, conjuring a story about his partner and co-star Oja Kodar and an incident involving Pablo Picasso, who himself noted: 'Art is a lie. A lie that makes us realize the truth.' (Rudyard Kipling's poem *The Conundrum of the Workshops*, with its refrain 'but is it Art?' also resonates throughout the film.)

With *F for Fake*, Welles left a document that finessed his mercurial image: provocateur, jester, charlatan, enigma. In life and work, Welles refused to conform. His final completed film is a testament to his uniqueness.

...THIS ISN'T A MOVIE THAT CAN BE JUDGED BY THE KINDS OF YARDSTICKS WE APPLY TO MOST OTHERS.

AMAZING GRACE

ALAN ELLIOTT (REALIZED BY),
SYDNEY POLLACK (UNCREDITED);
US; 1972/2018; 89 MINS

ALSO SEE

The Beatles: Get Back
(p.127)

A Great Day in Harlem
(Jean Bach; 1994)
A 1958 portrait of jazz musicians in
Harlem is the starting point for a
journey through that era.

Hoover Street Revival
(Sophie Fiennes; 2002)
A portrait of South Central L.A.'s Greater
Bethany Community Church and its
charismatic preacher Noel Jones.

What Happened, Miss Simone?
(Liz Garbus; 2015)
An unvarnished account of the life
of the singer-songwriter,
activist and firebrand.

This record of Aretha Franklin's extraordinary performances at the New Temple Missionary Baptist Church in Los Angeles on 13 and 14 January 1972 is no conventional concert film. They were a return to her roots – the gospel tradition that she grew up in. Footage of the events was kept in a vault for 35 years before director Alan Elliott, sound mixer Serge Perron and editor Jeff Buchanan employed advances in digital technology to piece this film together.

The audio recording of Franklin performing with her band, alongside the Southern California Community Choir under the musical direction of Alexander Hamilton, was the most successful album of the singer's career. Warner Bros. had commissioned director Sydney Pollack to film the event. However, with the crew unable to use clapperboards, the footage was not synched to the sound recording. Deemed unusable, Warner Bros. shelved it. In 2007, Elliott retrieved the footage and was able to digitally synch image and sound. With Buchanan, he pieced together highlights from both nights, occasionally picking alternate audio tracks to the ones that appeared on the original album. Franklin objected to the film's release and took legal action against it. It was eventually released following her death and with her family's blessing.

Amazing Grace bears witness to the power of Franklin's voice and magnetism. Elliott includes snatches of Pollack's backstage and rehearsal footage, seamlessly integrating it with the performance, sometimes even mid-song. He also makes much of emcee Reverend James Cleveland's charismatic presence and the choir – their call-and-response moments with Franklin emphasizing the ease she feels in this environment, as well as her command of both soul and gospel.

Just as the occasionally unsteady camerawork unintentionally captures odd surprises, particularly in the cutaways to a rapt audience (which included Mick Jagger and Charlie Watts, who were in town recording *Exile on Main St.* and attended the second night), the tempo of the editing and the crosscutting between Franklin, Cleveland and the choir adds immeasurably to the film's energy. If the singer's performance is the main draw of this film, *Amazing Grace* is also essential as a time-capsule of an era and an impressive example of modern technology's role in salvaging a 'lost' film.

A BIGGER SPLASH

JACK HAZAN; UK;
1973; 106 MINS

Jack Hazan's account of a period in British painter David Hockney's life captures the artist at work and in a state of emotional abjection following his split from artist, model and muse Peter Schlesinger. A fly-on-the-wall documentary, interspersed with semi-fictional scenes that articulate the artist's sense of loss and occasionally segue into moments of fantasy, *A Bigger Splash* takes place between 1971 and 1973, around the time Hockney completed 'Pool with Two Figures'. The film takes its name from the artist's iconic 1967 work and the film's aesthetic could be seen to absorb the thinking behind that work. As Hockney noted of his painting: 'I realize that a splash could never be seen this way in real life, it happens too quickly. And I was amused by this, so I painted it in a very, very slow way.'

Hazan, in tandem with his partner, co-writer and editor David Mingay, had approached Hockney with the idea of making a documentary portrait, but the artist initially declined. Nevertheless, Hazan went ahead. Notwithstanding occasional footage of Hockney at work, socializing and captured in private moments, *A Bigger Splash* mostly comprises the people in orbit around him. There are conversations – a combination of real and staged – between Hockney's friends, colleagues, gallerists and other artists. There are also appearances by Schlesinger, who became more involved in the project after Hazan agreed to pay him for his time.

Key to *A Bigger Splash* is a visual dialogue between Hockney, his subjects and his paintings. Hazan's camera captures him in the process of creation – and in one instance, destruction – just as he is reeling from his loss. Hockney seems unfocused in certain scenes; with the anchor that Schlesinger provided gone, the artist is adrift in the world. Later, Hazan imagines the emotional place Schlesinger might occupy now that he is no longer a part of his ex-lover's life. The film reconstructs Hockney's 1967 portrait *Beverly Hills Housewife*, with Schlesinger metaphorically locked outside of that world. The sequence also highlights a central theme of the film – the importance of surfaces; from mirrors and reflections in windows, to dapples of sunlight on pool water – textures that inform Hockney's work from this period. Blurring the line between documentary and fiction, Hazan creates a compelling portrait of an artist and his work that presaged the emergence of scripted reality series.

BURDEN OF DREAMS

LES BLANK; US;
1982; 95 MINS

Les Blank's account of the making of Werner Herzog's 1982 period drama *Fitzcarraldo* is one of the most compelling records of cinematic hubris. It wasn't the first documentary to focus on the creative process of feature film production, and many fine films followed in its wake. But it excels in its portrait of self-mythologizing, devil-may-care ambition facing off against the intransigency of the natural world.

Blank began his career making industrial films, but would become known for his documentaries exploring traditional American music forms. He first encountered Herzog when he made the short *Werner Herzog Eats His Shoe* (1980), in which the German filmmaker delivers on his wager with Errol Morris, following the latter's completion of his debut feature documentary *Gates of Heaven* (1978). Blank then found himself joining Herzog on the director's wildly ambitious feature project.

A fictional portrait of a nineteenth-century Peruvian rubber baron, *Fitzcarraldo*'s centrepiece saw an indigenous tribe, under the watchful eye of the near-maniacal industrialist, manually transport a ship over a small mountain between two rivers. The actual ship transported over a mountain had been considerably smaller and was disassembled before its journey across land. But Herzog's study in obsession – a reflection of his own wayward inclinations – required the behemoth remain intact.

Blank recorded the various obstacles that stalled the production over a period of years. A conflict between two tribes had forced Herzog to relocate the production. And Jason Robards, who was originally cast as Fitzcarraldo, bailed out due to illness. Along with him went Mick Jagger, who was cast as a second mate, and with his departure so went his character. Robards was replaced by Klaus Kinski, appearing in the fourth of five collaborations with Herzog. (The director's 1999 documentary *My Best Fiend*, about his relationship with Kinski, would highlight just how difficult his lead actor could be.)

The length and arduous nature of the *Fitzcarraldo* shoot became a trial for the introverted Blank, who wrote in his journal, 'I'm tired of it all and I couldn't care less if they move the stupid ship – or finish the fucking film'. But for all the trials Blank faced personally, his film is a stunning record of Herzog's determination to achieve his vision at all costs. *Burden of Dreams*, like *Fitzcarraldo*, acknowledges the cruel majesty of the natural world. But Blank's 'making-of' also finds in Herzog a figure crazed enough to rise to the challenge of overcoming it.

THE QUINCE TREE SUN

EL SOL DEL MEMBRILLO
VICTOR ERICE;
SPAIN; 1992; 133 MINS

It was perhaps inevitable that Victor Erice, whose small body of work is so perfectly framed and sensitive to the subtlest changes in light, should make a documentary about a painter. But in his intimate, meticulous and gently probing portrait of Antonio López García at work, Erice not only captures the Spanish artist grappling with the challenges of representation, he finds him engaging with notions of mortality, as embodied in the fruit hanging from the subject of his painting, a quince tree in the backyard of his studio.

Described by art critic Robert Hughes as 'the greatest realist artist alive', García has remained aloof from his peers, more attuned to the work of Italian Renaissance painters and Velásquez than contemporary trends. This is borne out in a conversation between García and a friend, as they discuss Michelangelo's *The Last Judgement*. García's fascination with a moment frozen in time is also reflected in Erice's work – *The Spirit of the Beehive* (1973) and *El Sur* (1983) – which capture the fragility of life in Spain under the rule of fascist dictator General Franco, and contain moments of such stillness they take on a painterly quality. But in *The Quince Tree Sun*, the challenge lies less in freezing a moment in time than in the moment passing too quickly.

The process of creation is twofold. We witness García's meticulous preparation for his painting; the draughtsman's skill at mapping out his terrain, attempting to faithfully document what he sees and deciding how to capture the everchanging quality of light. Then there is Erice's attempts to film García at work. He shot every day for two months and experienced the same problems as his subject when it came to variances in available light. And just as García expressed

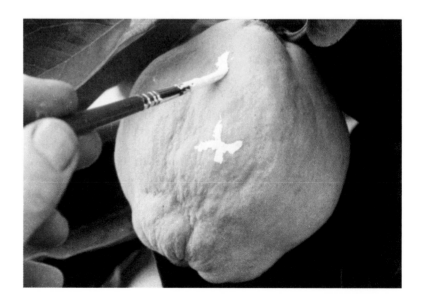

frustration at limitations due to the size of his canvas, Erice intermittently ran out of film and budget, and was forced at times to resort to video to continue shooting.

Time dominates the film. García's process requires too much of it and with the canvas far from complete, the fruit on the tree ripens too quickly for him. He has taken on a Sisyphean task and in the end, the only completed work of art is Erice's captivating minimalist portrait.

GERI

MOLLY DINEEN;
UK; 1999; 89 MINS

In 1999, Geri Halliwell – soon to be an ex-member of the country's biggest pop act, The Spice Girls – approached Molly Dineen to make an honest film about her life. Dineen agreed, but on one condition: that she had final cut. What emerges is a fascinating portrait of an individual desperate to escape the trappings of celebrity yet simultaneously addicted to it.

Having spent a decade exploring the eccentricities of British life and institutions, Dineen admits to a fascination with her subject from the outset: 'I find fame confusing now that it's such a growth industry. Increasingly, whatever you read, wherever you look, your attention is focused on celebrity. But we rarely get to see the real person unless there's a crisis.' When we first see Geri, aka Ginger Spice, recording herself in a Paris hotel the day after she decided to leave the band, she appears relatively calm. Two days later, Dineen arrives, curious about the singer's invitation. They discuss creative control of the film on a Eurostar back to London – Dineen retained control – where the filmmaker witnesses the first instance of Geri's public life when a middle-aged businessman asks her to autograph his shirt.

Dineen visits Geri's Hertfordshire retreat, a rented cottage on a farm, and meets her mother. They trawl through her personal belongings, with Geri narrating the story of her life. From there, they go to Sotheby's and a charity auction of her stage wardrobe, an audition for a role in a Bond film, to New York where Geri is announced as the Goodwill Ambassador for the United Nations Population Fund, and back to London for a show celebrating her friend Prince Charles' 50th birthday. Throughout, Dineen questions Geri about her motivations – why she claims to want a quiet life but cannot step out of the limelight.

Dineen's portrait is never cruel, but neither is it adulatory. Geri's attraction to fame appears driven by ambition and loneliness. The singer even admits that Dineen's presence was company for her, until she tires of all the questioning and effectively replaces the filmmaker with a dog. Made before the rise of social media, *Geri* may pale against more recent celebrity exposés. But coming just a few years after the death of Princess Diana, Dineen's film articulately – and often wittily – explores the precarious nature of life in the public eye.

ALSO SEE

Amy
(p.122)

Lily Tomlin
(Nick Broomfield, Joan Churchill; 1986)
A frank record of the US actor and comedian's preparation for her solo show.

Madonna: Truth or Dare
(Alek Keshishian; 1991)
The pop icon presents herself to the world as she prepares for her 'Blond Ambition' tour.

Actress
(Robert Greene; 2014)
Brandy Burre attempts to revive her screen career as Greene explores the complexity of a life lived as a performance.

I WANT INFORMALITY, I WANT CHARACTER, I WANT INTIMACY,

Molly Dineen

BUT I DON'T WANT LOSS OF DIGNITY.

THE GLEANERS AND I

LES GLANEURS ET LA GLANEUSE
AGNÈS VARDA;
FRANCE; 2000; 82 MINS

In the last two decades of her life, Agnès Varda's documentary work became as celebrated as her earlier narrative features. The renaissance was sparked by this singular travelogue, which found the filmmaker exploring the French countryside and its history in search of gleaners – individuals who gather food from the land. But her journey soon expands beyond the gleaning of fruit and vegetables, encompassing all kinds of objects, knowledge and even her own filmmaking process.

Opening with an appraisal of Jean-François Millet's 1857 painting *The Gleaners*, a portrait of three women gathering stray stalks of wheat, Varda begins her journey in the countryside, meeting a variety of people who scour the land for food discarded during a harvest. (A series of whimsical cutaways show advocates, in full regalia, quoting sections of the law that justify this practice.) From there, she encounters a Michelin-starred restauranteur whose cuisine only uses what the nearby land has to offer; artists who create their work from the discarded objects they find; homeless youths who vandalized a supermarket because of its policy of drenching discarded food in bleach; and city dwellers who forage markets. Among the latter is Alain F. who resides at a hostel in the Paris district of Montparnasse and teaches French to recently arrived immigrants. Varda's affection for him is palpable. In her 2002 follow-up, *The Gleaners and I: Two Years Later*, she meets him again and he reveals, with some consternation, that the first film made him a minor celebrity.

No sooner has the film started than Varda acknowledges her own role in this tradition, albeit as a gatherer of images. Working with digital for the first time, she delights in its portability and the ease by which she can 'glean' images of the world around her. (It's an idea she takes further in *Faces Places*, her joyful 2017 collaboration with the artist JR.) Varda's boundless curiosity makes *The Gleaners and I* a delight; whether it's her passion for heart-shaped potatoes – her favourite, placed on her mantlepiece, comes to represent her fascination with the ageing process – or her joy at seeing an unexpected shot of a lens cap, dancing in the air as it dangles from her camera. Contemplating art, the law and politics within the context of her subject, Varda's lust for life and unique perspective on the world make her the perfect travelling companion.

I DIDN'T HAVE A LIST OF GLEANERS HANDY.

Agnès Varda

I HAD TO FIND THEM.

SOME KIND OF MONSTER HAS AGED WELL . . .

PARTLY BECAUSE THERE'S BEEN NOTHING ELSE LIKE IT.

METALLICA: SOME KIND OF MONSTER

JOE BERLINGER,
BRUCE SINOFSKY; US; 2004;
141 MINS

Joe Berlinger and Bruce Sinofsky's film is a painstaking record of two tumultuous years in the life of the legendary metal group. It is also one of the funniest accounts of life in the rock world, with lead singer James Hetfield, drummer Lars Ulrich and lead guitarist Kirk Hammett unintentionally drawing comparisons with the hapless band members of Rob Reiner's beloved 1984 mockumentary *This is Spinal Tap*.

Formed in 1981, Metallica rose to become one of the world's most successful groups. But as a new century dawned, they began to unravel. Long-term bassist Jason Newsted departed. The band's opposition to the Napster peer-to-peer file sharing network garnered an uneasy fan response. And two decades of drink, drugs and touring had taken its toll. As a result, the band's management company brought in 'performance enhancement coach' Phil Towle to help them reconcile their differences and get them back to recording and touring. At the same time, the band agreed to allow Berlinger and Sinofsky (who they first encountered when they gave permission for the filmmakers to use their music for the 1996 documentary *Paradise Lost: The Child Murders at Robin Hood Hills*) to record the therapy sessions, their family life and the drawn-out rehearsal and recording sessions for what would become their 2003 album *St. Anger*, whose third track gave the film its title. However, no sooner had filming begun than Hetfield checked into a rehab clinic and was gone for a year. When he returned, he questioned the value of the film. These discussions eventually became part of the documentary.

The band are remarkably frank on camera. Such honesty, though refreshing, punctuates the film with unintended comedy. Ulrich's irony-free admiration for his art purchases, along with his exchanges with his hirsute father – who resembles a mystic more than a parent – are hilarious, as are Hammett's discussion of surfing and his 'lack' of ego. And Hetfield accompanying his daughter to a ballet class, along with his expressed desire to remain anonymous while driving an outrageously ostentatious car, are deadpan delights. There's also Towle's parade of garish jumpers and a scene featuring a Metallica-styled Christmas tree. Unintentional humour notwithstanding, the film is an unsparing portrait of a band overcoming personal demons in the interest of their collective endeavour; to reignite both their creativity – with a new bassist in tow – and the desire to play for their fans.

ALSO SEE

The Belovs
(p.40)

The Decline of Western Civilization Part II: The Metal Years
(Penelope Spheeris; 1988)
A spirited, warts-and-all portrait of L.A.'s heavy metal scene in the 1980s.

American Movie
(Chris Smith; 1999)
A hilarious account of a young filmmaker's attempt to make a low-budget horror movie.

Anvil! The Story of Anvil
(Sacha Gervasi; 2008)
The story of arguably the least successful metal band in history.

THE CONCERT
FILM

Although there were some early examples, most notably *Jazz on a Summer's Day* (1959), a record of the 1958 Newport Jazz Festival, and *The T.A.M.I. Show* (1964), which tapped into the rapidly expanding worlds of pop and soul, it wasn't until the rise of the counterculture in the US that the concert film really took shape.

If D.A. Pennebaker helped forge Bob Dylan's public persona with *Don't Look Back* (1967, p.94), the director's *Monterey Pop* (1968) captured the flower power movement at its height with a record of the 1967 Californian festival. It was followed by *Woodstock* (1970), Michael Wadleigh's era-defining film. However, unearthed footage of the 1969 Harlem Cultural Festival, brought together by Questlove for his euphoric and more politically tinged *Summer of Soul (...Or, When the Revolution Could Not Be Televised)* (2021) highlights a more diverse music landscape at that time than Wadleigh's film alone represented. If *Woodstock* was an optimistic highpoint of this era, the Maysles and Charlotte Zwerin's *Gimme Shelter* (1970) hinted at the dark days that lay ahead for US society. An experimental film, it captured the Rolling Stones' infamous gig at Altamont Speedway in 1969, which descended into chaos and violence, and murder. Another unearthed moment from this era, *Amazing Grace* (1972/2018, p.98), saw Aretha Franklin perform the gospel music from her youth in tandem with the soul that defined her career.

The concert film reached a high point with *The Last Waltz* (1978). Directed by Martin Scorsese, who was an editor on *Woodstock*, this record of The Band's last performance remains one of the greatest films in this genre and set the template for the many concert films that followed. At least, until *Stop Making Sense* (1984) came along. Jonathan Demme's film resembled performance theatre and inspired a new generation in challenging the conventions of the genre, from The Beastie Boys' *Awesome; I Fuckin' Shot That!* (2006), which gathered footage shot by fans, to Beyoncé's euphoric *Homecoming* (2019) , a record of her ambitious 2018 Coachella performance.

Opposite: *Summer of Soul (...Or, When the Revolution Could Not Be Televised)* (2021)
Above: *Gimme Shelter* (1970)

RIZE

DAVID LACHAPELLE;
US; 2005; 86 MINS

Dance represents an act of rebellion and form of escape in David LaChapelle's feature directorial debut, which focuses on a culture that grew out of Los Angeles' South Central neighbourhood. It details the challenges his subjects face living in one of the city's tougher neighbourhoods. However, the acclaimed photographer's trademark colour-saturated palette ultimately presents this story as a celebration of dance over adversity.

Opening with a montage of the Los Angeles riots of 1965 and 1992, the film cuts to Dragon, a local dancer, who acknowledges the troubles of the recent past: 'We were all kinds when this happened, but we managed to grow from these ashes.' He works with Thomas 'Tommy the Clown' Johnson, a charismatic figure in the neighbourhood who, after a time in prison, turned his life around, became a children's entertainer and initiated a syncopated dance style known as Clowning. His aim was to give young children and teenagers in the area another route into adulthood that didn't involve gang affiliation. The Clowning style – movement perfectly attuned to the rhythms of hip-hop – took off and eventually branched out into an alternative, more aggressive form, known as Krumping, whose speed prompted the inclusion of the text at the beginning of *Rize*: 'The footage in this film has not been sped up in any way.'

LaChapelle focuses on the key members of the two dance scenes, chronicling their home lives and the obstacles they overcome as they prepare for the fifth tournament between Clowners and Krumpers. While the community is forced to deal with the trauma of gang-related deaths and the daily struggle to survive, the film emphasizes the importance of dance and the camaraderie it generates. In doing so, it challenges lazy racial stereotypes. As Dragon explains: 'This is not about a bunch of people acting wild. This is an art form, just as valid as your ballet, as your waltz, as your tap dance, except we wouldn't have to go to school for this 'cause it was already implanted in us. From birth.' *Rize* ends on a euphoric note, with an extended dance sequence. Playing out to the jubilant sound of the Edwin Hawkins Singers' rendition of 'Oh Happy Day', LaChapelle's rich, lustrous camerawork captures his subjects' bodies in glorious motion.

ALSO SEE

Pina
(p.120)

Dogtown and the Z-Boys
(Stacy Peralta; 2001)
A history of a skateboarding and an outlaw crew on the streets of Santa Monica and Venice Beach.

This is the Life
(Ava DuVernay; 2008)
A portrait of the Good Life Cafe, which became a centre of L.A.'s alternate hip-hop and rap culture in the 1990s.

Sonita
(Rokhsareh Ghaemmaghami; 2015)
A young Afghan refugee in Iran uses her skills as a rapper to rail against the life she is expected to lead.

MAN ON WIRE

JAMES MARSH;
UK/US; 2008; 94 MINS

Often referred to as one of the great crimes of art, Philippe Petit's extraordinary high-wire walk between the Twin Towers of the World Trade Center early on 7 August 1974 took on new resonance following the 9/11 terrorist attacks. Drawing heavily from Petit's 2002 book *To Reach the Clouds*, James Marsh's film is a thrilling story, all the more remarkable for there being no footage of what took place beyond a handful of photographs.

Producer Simon Chinn first conceived of a documentary about Petit's achievement when he heard him speak on BBC Radio 4's *Desert Island Discs* show. After gaining Petit's consent, Chinn contacted James Marsh, who had impressed the producer with his unsettling 1999 docu-drama *Wisconsin Death Trip*. Meetings between Petit and Marsh resulted in the filmmaker writing a detailed outline that placed the French wire-walker at the centre of a group who approached their ambitious venture like a heist.

Footage of Petit's previous achievements – walking between the two towers of Notre Dame cathedral in Paris and the two north pylons of Sydney Harbour Bridge – are included as a preamble to the main event. As the team prepare, *Man on Wire* gradually increases tension by detailing the intricacies involved in planning the stunt. Successfully evading security checks at the entrance to the World Trade Center, carrying equipment up 110 floors to the roof and passing the cable between the two towers by means of a bow and arrow, was a combination of inspiration, luck and steadfast belief in the enterprise.

Petit is a fine storyteller, combining roguish charm with an impressive recollection of how he felt as the walk neared. The film excels in combining interviews alongside a portrait of New York and the US in the 1970s. Watergate was tearing apart the legitimacy of Nixon's presidency, while corruption was rife within New York's administration. Petit's walk was a reminder to New Yorkers of how their city, at its best, could inspire wonder. (Although the 2001 attacks on the towers are not directly referenced in the film, knowledge of that event adds a mournful layer to it.) Ultimately, *Man on Wire* is testament to a particular kind of genius – of someone who broke the law in order to give us something to marvel at.

THE BEACHES OF AGNÈS

LES PLAGES D'AGNÈS
AGNÈS VARDA; FRANCE;
2008; 112 MINS

At the age of 80, Agnès Varda chose to turn her camera fully on herself. 'I'm playing the role of a little old lady,' she notes as the film begins, 'pleasantly plump and talkative, telling her life story.' Then she adds, 'And yet, it's others I'm interested in, others I like to film'. Always the most generous of artists, Varda's autobiographical cine-essay is a journey through her life via the people she encountered. And at its heart lies a love story.

It begins on the French coast. Varda notes: 'If we opened me up we'd find beaches'. Aided by her crew, she erects an array of mirrors that will allow her to 'reflect' on the past. From there, she describes her youth, a chance encounter that resulted in her becoming a photographer and, eventually, a filmmaker. Her debut was the coastal drama *La Pointe Courte* (1955), which pre-dated the arrival of the French New Wave yet bore all the hallmarks of this radical new cinema. She visits the small fishing town where she shot the film and is reunited with locals who appeared in it. Varda's ease in the company of others, an enthusiasm for their different ways of living and perspectives on life, has long been one of the pleasures of her work.

As she progresses through her various film projects and journeys, Varda's joy at remembering them is tempered by sadness at the loss of friends and colleagues. An exhibition of her work with a theatre company in Avignon is particularly poignant. Nevertheless, Varda remains a playful narrator of her life; her walking backwards in various scenarios becomes a recurring motif for the journey she is taking in time and an acknowledgement that to do so prevents one from seeing the full picture.

The Beaches of Agnès is no conventional biographical account of Varda's life, but she reveals so much about herself in the way she tells it. Nowhere is this more evident than in her discussion of her husband, filmmaker Jacques Demy. He lies at the heart of the film. She had already explored his youth with the glorious *Jacquot de Nantes* (1991). With *The Beaches of Agnès*, she gives us both their stories, bound together, in life, love and art.

THIS IS CINEMA IN CINEMA,

Agnès Varda

AND MEMORY INTO AN ACTION.

THE SEPTEMBER ISSUE

R.J. CUTLER;
US; 2009; 90 MINS

ALSO SEE

The Queen of Versailles
(p.76)

Unzipped
(Douglas Keeve; 1995)
A record of New York fashion prodigy
Isaac Mizrahi's preparations for the
launch of his Fall 1994 collection.

Page One: Inside the New York Times
(Andrew Rossi; 2010)
A pivotal year in the life of the
iconic newspaper as it battles a
nascent online culture.

Diana Vreeland: The Eye Has to Travel
(Lisa Immordino Vreeland,
Bent-Jorgen Perlmutt,
Frédéric Tcheng; 2011)
A portrait of the influential
Harper's Bazaar and *Vogue* editor.

Would R.J. Cutler's behind-the-scenes documentary have garnered as much interest had *The Devil Wears Prada* (2006) not preceded it? That hit film was adapted from Lauren Weisberger's roman à clef about her experiences as an assistant to *Vogue* editor-in-chief Anna Wintour. Cutler's film follows Wintour as her team prepares the publication of the September 2007 issue, the largest in the magazine's history. However, in expanding his focus to include other figures, most notably the magazine's influential Creative Director Grace Coddington, Cutler's film becomes a fascinating examination of how creativity survives within a ruthless, profit-driven industry.

The September issue of *Vogue*, as its Executive Fashion Director Candy Pratts Price notes, is 'January in fashion' – the most important issue of the year. From the outset, Cutler makes clear the pivotal role Wintour exerts over every aspect of the magazine, which she has presided over since 1988. (When Price comments that *Vogue* employees belong to the 'church of fashion' and Cutler inquires whether Wintour is its high priestess, Price responds, 'I would say pope'.) Cutler introduces Wintour in close-up, without her signature sunglasses, perhaps implying that the film intends to peel away the veneer of her public image. However, she remains guardedly conscious of every word she speaks and gesture she makes. Given access to the inner chambers of the fashion world, Cutler emphasizes the magnitude of Wintour and *Vogue*'s reach, not so much reflecting the shifts in fashion – what colours or styles are in or out – as playing a key role in deciding them. But it's with the increasing presence of Coddington that the film shifts gear and sparks with energy.

Wintour acknowledges the importance of Coddington, but also admits to their combative dynamic; nowhere more so than in Coddington's constant despair over the editor's trimming of her painstakingly organized and choreographed fashion shoots. Cutler clearly admires Coddington's imagination. (In one lovely scene of spontaneity, she decides to include cinematographer Bob Richman in a shoot, but even then she has to fight to ensure his paunch is not airbrushed.) He also recognizes the importance of this relationship. The inclusion of Coddington, as inspiring as she is irascible, elevates *The September Issue* above most other documentaries about the fashion world.

EXIT THROUGH THE GIFT SHOP

BANKSY;
UK; 2010; 87 MINS

Thierry Guetta is the subject of this hilarious record of one man's transformation from chronicler of an art movement to dubious practitioner. It starts out with Guetta wanting to film a British street artist at work, but the creative roles are soon reversed. Or as subject-turned-director Banksy frames it: 'The film is what happened when this guy tried to make a documentary about me. But he was actually a lot more interesting than I am. So now the film is about him.'

Guetta spent years filming every moment of his life, from raising his children to whatever events unfold on the streets of L.A. An encounter with his cousin, street artist Space Invader, sees him change focus. Guetta attempts to contact Banksy who, though initially suspicious of the Frenchman, is eventually won over by his enthusiasm and invites him into his circle of friends and collaborators. Guetta helps the pseudonymous artist on his successful Los Angeles debut and even embarks on a jaunt to place a provocative Bansky artwork in Disneyland – an act that sees Guetta apprehended by the park's security, further earning the artist's respect.

But Guetta's attempts as a filmmaker prove an incomprehensible and unwatchable mess. At this point, Bansky seizes control of the camera and directs this film. Undeterred in his creative ambitions, Guetta draws on his experiences with various street artists to reinvent himself as Mr. Brainwash, creating his own mass-produced images. He even hosts a sprawling L.A. show of his rapidly produced and highly derivative work. Banksy charts this transformation, but in the film's closing moments makes clear his opinion of the new street art star and his endeavours: 'Andy Warhol made his statement by repeating famous icons until they became meaningless. But he was extremely iconic in the way that he did it... Thierry really made them meaningless.'

Banksy emerges as a laconically funny guide to Guetta's rise (his to-camera addresses resemble one of the fictional vox-pop characters from the UK TV satire *Charlie Brooker's Screenwipe*), highlighting the fickle relationship between art and commerce, while also assembling a fascinating overview of street art's emergence as a politically and socially potent form. But it's the friendly-turned-fractious relationship between the artist and Guetta that makes the film so engaging, even if its effect on Banksy ultimately proved dispiriting: 'I always used to encourage everyone I met to make art. I think everyone should do it. I don't really do that so much anymore.'

THE FILM IS THE END OF MY PUBLIC LIFE RATHER THAN THE BEGINNING.

Banksy

PINA

WIM WENDERS;
GERMANY/FRANCE/UK/US;
2011; 103 MINS

In his heartfelt tribute to Pina Bausch, Wim Wenders embraces 3D technology as a way to enhance the cinematic power of the iconic German choreographer's most acclaimed dance pieces. It's one of many elements in a documentary that revels in the textured nature of performance and, ultimately, film itself. A memorial and a celebration, Wenders' collaboration with Tanztheater Wuppertal, Bausch's company, underpins her belief in dance as both an artistic act and a reflection on life. As Bausch notes in footage that appears in the film: 'Dance comes in when words aren't enough.'

Pina opens, ends and is punctuated throughout with a performance of Bausch's 1982 piece *The Nelken Line*, which begins on stage before relocating to the streets of Wuppertal and the surrounding countryside. Woven between these and other impromptu dance sequences are performances of four major works: *The Rite of Spring* (1975), *Café Müller* (1978), *Kontakthof* (1978–2008) and *Vollmond* (2006). None is featured in its entirety and each cuts to testimonies from members of Bausch's troupe. Wenders recorded their audio separately from filming them, giving the impression that we are listening to their thoughts. (He employed a similar device, to stunning effect, in his 1987 drama *Wings of Desire*.) It's both playful and highly effective, particularly when the lead female dancer of *The Rite of Spring* admits, 'Meeting Pina was like finding a language finally'; she acknowledges the belief that Bausch sought in her work a way to connect on a purely physical, existential level. And Wenders' shifting the dances from the stage to locations around Wuppertal erases the line between art and life. Bausch's final statement in the film, 'Dance, dance, otherwise we are lost', is rendered throughout by the company interacting with the everyday environments, whether its dancing on a concrete island as cars pass by, or beneath and aboard the city's suspension railway.

Wenders makes the most of close-ups and multiple perspectives, and the use of 3D technology feels integral to his vision. Like Werner Herzog's equally inspiring *Cave of Forgotten Dreams* (2010), Wenders employs 3D as a way to explore and emphasize depth of field. Veils shimmer as dancers pass through them and the staging of each piece resonates more vibrantly – matching the energy of the choreography. Wenders' camera marvels at the way dancers move and interact. It's a joy for those familiar with Bausch's work and a thrilling introduction for the uninitiated.

ALSO SEE

Paris is Burning
(p.37)

On Tour with Pina Bausch
(Chantal Akerman; 1983)
A profile of the choreographer and her work during a tour of Germany, Italy and France.

Towards Mathilde
(Claire Denis; 2005)
A spare, understated record of French choreographer Mathilde Monnier at work on a new dance project.

Cunningham
(Alla Kovgan; 2019)
A celebration of the influential dancer and choreographer, with landmark dance pieces captured in 3D.

AMY

ASIF KAPADIA; UK; 2015;
128 MINS

Asif Kapadia's portrait of British singer-songwriter Amy Winehouse continues the style of 'true fiction' he refined with his propulsive 2010 sports documentary *Senna*. But whereas that film focused primarily on the Brazilian racing driver's career, *Amy* employs intimate footage shot by family, friends and lovers, alongside studio and live recordings, to portray a life full of potential that ended tragically as a result of excessive substance abuse.

An exhaustive account of Winehouse's brief life, suggesting failings of those close to her, *Amy* sensitively balances the events that led to her death with a celebration of her extraordinary talent. The first half of the film charts Winehouse's rise. She is in her mid-teens when we first see her, filmed at a friend's birthday party. Already fronting the National Youth Jazz Orchestra, her voice sounds far beyond her years. Signing with Island Records, its president Nick Gatfield describes her as 'a force of nature'. The intensity of Winehouse's feelings and experiences find their way into her lyrics, which are sharp as a blade yet delivered with cool detachment. Kapadia uses them, often written on screen, to propel the narrative and as an expression of the singer's inner emotional state.

As Winehouse's allegiances shift – her circle of friends is replaced by people too invested in her commercial success – and her dependence on drink and drugs increases, Kapadia's focus widens, highlighting the role played by sustained media attention and an air of schadenfreude among the general public in exacerbating the singer's fragile condition. Her mercurial nature becomes more pronounced and her appearances increasingly chaotic. Winehouse's father Mitch and her ex-husband Blake Fielder-Civil are presented as unwitting agents in the singer's decline, the alleged callousness of their actions looming larger in hindsight.

As with *Senna*, Kapadia accompanies the footage with recollections and observations by those close to Winehouse, from childhood and former friends to family members and collaborators. Notwithstanding the sadness of how her life ended, *Amy* never loses sight of her gift. Winehouse's passion for music is witnessed, just months before her death, in a studio rehearsal with her idol Tony Bennett. In a subsequent interview, he suggests that she should be remembered alongside Ella Fitzgerald and Billie Holiday. It's a fitting tribute to an incandescent talent.

ALSO SEE

The Beatles: Get Back
(p.127)

Marlene
(Maximilian Schell; 1984)
An audio interview, with an archive of visuals, finds the iconic star irascible in detailing her life.

Let's Get Lost
(Bruce Weber; 1988)
An intimate portrait of the brilliant but troubled jazz trumpeter and singer Chet Baker.

Ingrid Bergman: In Her Own Words
(Stig Björkman; 2015)
The Swedish film star's life is explored through the trove of home movies.

MY AIM WAS TO MAKE A FILM ABOUT WHO SHE REALLY WAS.

Asif Kapadia

FURTHER BEYOND

JOE LAWLOR, CHRISTINE
MOLLOY; IRELAND; 2016;
89 MINS

Part cine-essay, part visual travelogue, *Further Beyond* grapples with the pitfalls inherent in the biopic by unravelling the nature of factual storytelling. At the same time, it details the life of an eighteenth-century explorer, alongside the more recent history of co-creator Joe Lawlor's mother Helen. Provocative, witty and wilfully resistant to the trappings of genre, Lawlor and Christine Molloy's film gleefully defies any easy categorization.

Produced during a stop-gap between two narrative features by the duo, who also go by the name The Desperate Optimists, *Further Beyond* opens by stating the intention to produce a historical biopic, only for their documentary to end on that drama's opening scene. In between, actors Denise Gough and Alan Howley are seen recording voiceover commentaries that guide us through the proposed drama's various narrative strands. It focuses on Ambrose O'Higgins, an Irishman who made his way to Chile and became governor in the late eighteenth century. But *Further Beyond* is interspersed with asides questioning the mechanics of storytelling and the filmmaking process, the nature of representation, and the challenges of certain genres. There is also the story of young Helen Lawlor's journeys back and forth across the Atlantic. References to William Carlos Williams, Roland Barthes, Susan Sontag and Walter Benjamin combine with discussion of ethnographic director Robert Flaherty's work and the New York of Elia Kazan's *On the Waterfront* (1954) to dazzling effect, raising questions about the construct of narrative cinema. The two actors also enter this playful fray. Howley has a conversation with a young boy about his voiceover and later proposes to the unseen directors the possibility of his playing O'Higgins, should the biopic ever be made.

Lawlor and Molloy's narrative films, particularly their feature debut *Helen* (2008), skirt the boundaries of documentary. Here the reverse takes place. Sharing the same reservations about the biopic that novelist Laurent Binet's *HHhH* (2010) expressed about the biography, *Further Beyond* questions the possibility of creating a film that would satisfy the directors. (As Howley's commentary notes at one point, 'Certain genres set alarm bells off for us and the biopic is one of them'.) But the film is no dry academic exercise. Mischievous, imaginative and undaunted in its desire to find a new way of engaging with cinema, it is a marvel of invention.

ALSO SEE

News From Home
(p.34)

Valparaiso
(Joris Ivens; 1963)
Ivens and writer Chris Marker explore the Chilean city's present and colourful past.

Robinson in Space
(Patrick Keiller; 1997)
Paul Scofield's narrator and his friend explore the UK through its social, political and industrial history.

Four Corners
(James Benning; 1998)
The experimental filmmaker explores identity, history and place at the intersection of four US states.

IT'S A MEDITATION ON EMIGRATION AND TRAVEL,

Christine Molloy

THAT'S EXPLORED THROUGH A PECULIARLY IRISH EXPERIENCE.

DAWSON CITY: FROZEN TIME

BILL MORRISON; US; 2016;
120 MINS

In 1978, development in the Yukon's second largest city uncovered a landfill containing hundreds of reels of pre-sound Hollywood films. Found beneath the permafrost of a decommissioned swimming pool, the discovery forms the basis of Bill Morrison's fascinating documentary. Exploring this area's rich past and transforming the surviving footage into a phantasmagoria of moving images and apparitions, Morrison presents a fascinating history of early cinema and American life.

In the first decades of the twentieth century, Dawson City had been the last stop for Hollywood movies. It was cheaper for studios to leave the reels of celluloid there than have them shipped back to Los Angeles. Initially stored in a bank vault, the reels eventually became landfill for a sports and recreation building's foundations. On occasion, pieces of the highly flammable nitrate film surfaced and were set alight by children. Over 500 reels were eventually salvaged. Most existed in some state of disrepair; perfect material for Morrison, whose work has focused on transforming damaged films into hypnotic artworks.

Originally conceived as a short film, Morrison's investigation into the city's rich cultural and social history, aided by local museum and national park employees Kathy Jones and Michael Gates, soon expanded the scope of the project. Combining the uncovered footage with other archive material, including Eric Hegg's photographs of the Gold Rush – the discovery of an invaluable cache of his wet plate negatives is one of the film's many surprising tales – alongside present-day interviews, Morrison interweaves the region's sudden and turbulent growth in the late nineteenth-century with the history of early Hollywood. After all, Dawson City was where entertainment empresarios Sid Grauman and Alexander Pantages made their fortune, as well as Donald Trump's grandfather.

Dawson City's story would make a fascinating film in its own right, but Morrison's use of the discovered footage transforms it into something unique. Like *Decasia* (2002), a meditation on the beauty of decaying film and Morrison's most celebrated work, *Dawson City: Frozen Time* celebrates the aesthetic beauty of the medium. Morrison said that his film is 'a tale about the American twentieth century'. It is also a paean to the images created by a flickering light.

ALSO SEE

Nanook of the North
(p.160)

Decasia
(Bill Morrison; 2002)
MoMorrison's breakthrough film employs fragments of early film to create a hypnotic reverie.

My Winnipeg
(Guy Maddin; 2007)
Maddin draws on the aesthetics of early cinema to map out a history of the city he grew up in.

Henri-Georges Clouzot's Inferno
(Serge Bromberg; 2009)
A revered film preservationist reconstructs the French filmmaker's unfinished psychodrama.

THE BEATLES: GET BACK

PETER JACKSON;
UK/NEW ZEALAND/US;
2021; 468 MINUTES

ALSO SEE

Don't Look Back
(p.94)

One Plus One
(Jean-Luc Godard; 1968)
The French New Wave filmmaker
contrasts social unrest with the Rolling
Stones in a recording studio.

Rolling Thunder Revue
(Martin Scorsese; 2019)
A sprawling, immersive account of Bob
Dylan's ambitious, carnivalesque and
star-studded 1975 concert tour.

*Summer of Soul (...Or, When the
Revolution Could Not Be Televised)*
(Questlove; 2021)
This record of the 1969 Harlem Cultural
Festival contrasts sharply with other
concert films from the era.

More a reconstruction than a remake, Peter Jackson revisits the copious footage shot by Michael Lindsay-Hogg for *Let It Be* (1969), which caught The Beatles at the peak of their creative brilliance but also on the brink of separation. With a running time almost six times the length of the original film, *The Beatles: Get Back* presents a more complex account of the relationship between John, Paul, George and Ringo, revealing the deep well of love and respect that existed between the band members, even as their relationship was becoming increasingly fractious.

Jackson had previously employed colour, sound and 3D imagery to capture an age gone by in an altogether new way for his First World War documentary *They Shall Not Grow Old* (2018). Here, he uses digital technology to give the footage a sense of immediacy, as though it was shot only yesterday. The filmmaker edited the 60-plus hours of film – and almost twice as much audio – into chronological order, interspersed with judiciously chosen archive footage showing earlier incarnations of the group. The change in recording locations gives the filmmaker a natural break. The first part unfolds in a cavernous film studio in Twickenham. It culminates in a lunchtime announcement by George Harrison that he is leaving the band. Part two finds George back in the fold, but the band and their entourage have moved to the basement studio at Apple, their company headquarters on Savile Row. The mood is lighter and the band's larkiness shines through. In the final part, John, Paul, George and Ringo prepare for and give their live performance, on the rooftop of Apple's offices.

The film's length allows Jackson to capture the minutiae of the band's working relationship and creative process. What unfolds highlights both individual brilliance and collective harmony. Paul comes up with the riff that will eventually become 'Get Back', but it's the others' input that gives it shape. Their personalities complement as much as they clash. And the differences that eventually result in the band's demise, across each day, are less a record of mutual antipathy than frustration and a note of sadness that the end is near. But when they play together, particularly in the climactic rooftop gig, they are a band whose energy, charisma and brilliance is beyond question and who, for almost a decade, had the world at their feet.

HISTORY &

CONFLICT

THE WAR GAME

PETER WATKINS; UK; 1965;
47 MINS

ALSO SEE

Lessons of Darkness
(p.141)

Crossroads
(Bruce Conner; 1976)
The American artist collates footage
from the 700 cameras that recorded
the first two atomic tests, which took
place at Bikini Atoll.

The Atomic Cafe
(Jayne Loader, Kevin Rafferty,
Pierce Rafferty; 1982)
Propaganda created during the Cold War
is reconstructed to highlight a decades-
long campaign of misinformation.

Atomic: Living in Dread and Promise
(Mark Cousins; 2015)
Comprising a rich assembly of archive
material, this visual essay considers
the legacy of Hiroshima.

Detailing the lead-up to and aftermath of a nuclear attack, the reputation of *The War Game* has only increased with time. A pacifist treatise that presents a comprehensive argument against the proliferation of nuclear arms, Peter Watkins' concise and chilling film received an Academy Award and was acclaimed internationally, but proved so controversial in the UK it would not be screened on television for two decades.

The film opens with news reporting on increased tensions in Southeast Asia. Events rapidly escalate, impacting the tenuous relationship between East and West in Europe, culminating in the US and USSR launching simultaneous nuclear attacks. A bomb aimed at a Royal Air Force base in Kent instead falls on the nearby town of Rochester. Those not killed in the immediate blast or subsequent firestorm gradually succumb to the effects of radiation, malnutrition and violence from the resulting chaos. Asking 'would the survivors envy the dead?', the film ends on the despairing faces of children who question what future there is for them and a church congregation commemorating Christmas with a sobering rendition of 'Silent Night'.

Watkins was commissioned to make *The War Game* – originally planned as his first film but postponed because of its incendiary subject matter – following the success of his docu-drama *Culloden* (1964), which re-enacted the 1746 battle between Scottish Jacobites and the British Army. For his second feature, he drew on detailed reports of aerial attacks on German cities and reporting on the effects of the atomic detonations over Hiroshima and Nagasaki during the Second World War. He also incorporated official British government procedures that should be adopted in the event of a nuclear strike, to highlight their ineffectiveness.

Like *Culloden, The War Game* employs a reportage style. It blends harrowing docu-dramatizations alongside genuine vox-pop interviews with the British public, questioning their knowledge of precautions to be taken in the event of a nuclear attack. The film so alarmed the BBC that they decided to cancel the film's transmission. Watkins resigned, claiming government interference. The broadcaster denied any collusion, but papers released some 50 years later reveal how closely high-ranking ministers and heads at the BBC worked together to ban the film, fearful that it would cause widespread panic among the British populace. It finally aired on British television in 1985 and is now regarded as an essential and unerringly accurate portrayal of what the world might look like in the aftermath of a nuclear conflict.

I WAS TRYING TO SUGGEST THAT

MANKIND CAN SET LOOSE SOMETHING ENTIRELY BEYOND THE HUMAN ABILITY TO CONTROL.

Peter Watkins

THE SORROW AND THE PITY

LE CHAGRIN ET LA PITIÉ
MARCEL OPHÜLS;
SWITZERLAND/WEST GERMANY;
1969; 251 MINS

Banned on French television for over a decade, but now regarded as an essential record of a dark period in France's recent past, Marcel Ophüls' film was one of the first works in any medium to overturn myths regarding French involvement in the Second World War. Detailing the relationship between the Vichy government and Nazi Germany, the film draws from 50 hours of interviews and extensive archive footage, newsreels and propaganda, to detail the way collaboration, compromise and collusion became a way of life.

The town of Clermont-Ferrand is 20 miles from Vichy. The primary focus of Ophüls' film, it represents a microcosm of occupied France. Divided into two parts, 'The Collapse' and 'The Choice', *The Sorrow and the Pity* maps out the role played by residents and occupying troops in daily life, and against the wider landscape of the conflict. It details the speed with which France capitulated to the invading force, identifying in the town disparate voices that represented the fracturing attitudes towards the Nazis. Alongside those who abhorred everything Hitler and his forces stood for were anti-Communists who welcomed the Fascists and anti-Semites who informed on Jews living locally. Some wealthy, landed aristocracy and industrialists felt they had too much to lose, while others were soured by the impact of the First World War. But among those more pliant to the Nazi occupation were individuals who bravely found a way to resist both the Germans and their Vichy puppets.

A brisk film despite its long running time, Ophüls interviews a wide range of people who defend the position they took. There's the aristocrat who saw Nazi ideology as philosophically desirable but who found the uniform repulsive; a former teacher who can barely mask the delight they felt at the arrest of Jewish colleagues; an English undercover agent, worrying he would be labelled a coward because of his homosexuality, who joins the Resistance but then falls in love with a Nazi. There's also discussion of Anglo-French relations and how this fed into pro-Nazi sentiment. Ophüls' sardonic humour is ever-present, particularly in the way he undermines the credibility of certain claims with archive footage or the testimony of individuals beyond reproach. Throughout, he makes clear that the majority of French people didn't collaborate so much as try to carry on with their lives regardless. But even that assertion challenged the more palatable narrative that had been embraced in French society and which this film so thoroughly challenges.

ALSO SEE

State Funeral
(p.152)

Hôtel Terminus
(Marcel Ophüls; 1988)
A detailed portrait of the Gestapo Chief of Lyon, his crimes and his life after the Second World War.

Blind Spot: Hitler's Secretary
(André Heller,
Othmar Schmiderer; 2002)
An interview with Traudl Junge, who was Adolf Hitler's personal secretary from 1942 to 1945.

Final Account
(Luke Holland; 2021)
The surviving members of the Third Reich highlight the dangers of complacency towards extremist ideology.

THE WORLD AT WAR

JEREMY ISAACS (PRODUCER);
UK; 1973-74; 1,352 MINS

ALSO SEE

Shoah
(p.138)

Why We Fight
(Frank Capra; 1942–45)
A series of seven influential propaganda
documentaries produced by the
US Department of War.

Fires Were Started
(Humphrey Jennings; 1943)
A riveting account of firefighters battling
the London Blitz in the early years of
the Second World War.

They Shall Not Grow Old
(Peter Jackson; 2018)
First World War footage from the
Imperial War Museum is radically
transformed by technology.

The World at War was a landmark 26-episode series chronicling events that led to the outbreak of the Second World War, its expansion around the world and its toll upon soldiers and civilians alike. It was the most expensive factual series produced at that time and became the standard by which televised historical documentaries were judged.

Jeremy Isaacs had been working in current affairs broadcasting for 15 years when he began developing the series. His template was the BBC's *The Great War* (1964), which presented the 1914–18 conflict through a combination of archive footage, testimony and staged recreations. The Imperial War Museum, the technical adviser on that series, had been unhappy with the staged sequences, so when Isaacs approached it for help, he agreed to use only first-hand testimony and archive footage. Noble Frankland, the director of the museum, offered guidance on the structure, suggesting 15 major campaigns that deserved their own episode. Isaacs then added 11 more episodes, which detailed the political landscape out of which the conflict arose, life on the Allied domestic front and under occupation, the various ideologies at play and the persecution of peoples that resulted from them, and the world that eventually emerged from the chaos.

In contrast to the limited visual coverage of earlier conflicts, Isaacs had access to thousands of hours of footage from the various campaigns, occupied territories and home fronts, creating a rich and expansive record of the era. Passage through the conflict via major events and individual chapters focusing on specific topics gives the series coherence, but it is the testimonies of former soldiers and prisoners, civilians, politicians and journalists that give it emotional depth and add a personal dimension to the grand narrative. This works particularly well in detailing the rise of Hitler in Germany and the countries his forces occupied, as well as in conveying life in an increasingly militaristic Japan, and the domestic front in Britain and the US. (The episode dealing with the persecution of Jews would have been powerful at the time, but has since been surpassed by Claude Lanzmann's *Shoah* (p.138) and other documentaries). Laurence Olivier's narration and Carl Davis' score were the final key elements added by Isaacs in creating this engrossing historical record, which remains one of the most authoritative overviews of the conflict.

WE ACTUALLY SEE THE COUNTRY

CRACKING OPEN.

Pauline Kael, *The New Yorker*

THE BATTLE OF CHILE

LA BATALLA DE CHILE
PATRICIO GUZMÁN;
VENEZUELA/FRANCE/CUBA/CHILE;
1975–79; 359 MINS

Patricio Guzmán's account of Chile's descent, from a democratically elected leftist government into the chaos that resulted from the emergence of General Augusto Pinochet's right-wing military dictatorship, remains one of the pivotal works of revolutionary cinema. Dividing events into three parts, which reflect key moments from this turbulent era, Guzmán's film is a riveting on-the-ground account of a democracy stolen by right-wing forces.

Part one, 'Insurrection of the Bourgeoisie' unfolds in March 1973, before and after the re-election of Salvador Allende's Popular Unity party. The nation remains divided between leftist and right-wing parties. Guzmán captures the feeling on the streets, along with political events, demonstrations and the escalating violence. The film ends with newsreel footage of Argentine cameraman Leonardo Henrichsen filming street skirmishes and the shot from a soldier's rifle that kills him. Part two, 'The Coup d'État', unfolds a few months later, as the military attempt to wrest power from the democratically elected government. It initially fails, but a CIA-funded truck strike gradually suffocates the government and another coup, culminating in the bombing of the governmental palace, succeeds. Part three, 'The Power of the People', was completed six years after the coup and returns to the events that led to the political chaos documented in the first two parts.

The film's power derives from its immediacy. Guzmán and his crew throw themselves into the melee of a divided country. Interviews with people from all walks of life capture the urgency felt on both sides of the political divide, before witnessing the hope of democracy fade – we're never in doubt as to where Guzmán's loyalties lie – with the arrival of the military. In returning to events before the first two films for the third part, Guzmán grapples with the failure of the left to maintain power.

The filmmaker continued to tackle Chile's political strife for the next two decades. His first visit to the country since his self-imposed exile was documented in his cine-essay *Chile, the Obstinate Memory* (1997), its style bridging his urgent earlier work with his more ruminative *Nostalgia for the Light* (2010, p.74). That 1997 film features a record of the first domestic screening of *The Battle of Chile* and a discussion with those involved in its making. They pay tribute to cameraman Jorge Müller Silva, who worked on the films and was one of the many victims of Pinochet's regime, a reminder of the horrors that Guzmán's country experienced.

HEARTS AND MINDS

PETER DAVIS;
US; 1974; 112 MINS

ALSO SEE

Waltz with Bashir
(p.146)

In the Year of the Pig
(Emile de Antonio; 1968)
One of the first significant US films
to take a stand against the
Vietnam conflict.

The War at Home
(Glenn Silber, Barry Alexander
Brown; 1979)
A record of the anti-Vietnam War
movement in Madison, Wisconsin.

The Fog of War
(Errol Morris; 2003)
A probing, feature-length interview
with former US Secretary of Defense
(1961–68) Robert McNamara.

If political powers in the lead-up to and during the Second World War saw cinema as a successful platform for mass propaganda, by the time the Vietnam conflict was in full flow it had become an equally potent political tool in the hands of those opposing the state. Peter Davis' Academy Award-winning documentary, made while the war still raged, is a case in point. Although it divided opinions, its critique of the situation in Vietnam proved damning and contributed to the growing dissatisfaction among the US populace of their government's continued involvement in the 'police action'.

Davis' film lifts its title from one of President Johnson's more famous remarks about the conflict: 'We must be prepared to fight in Vietnam, but the ultimate victory will depend on the hearts and minds of the people who actually live out there.' The film juxtaposes footage of daily life for Vietnamese civilians during the conflict and interviews with local government officials, with testimonies from figures in the US military – current and former soldiers, as well as brass – and civilian advisers.

The opposing views on US involvement in Vietnam are most clearly represented by the Pentagon Papers whistle-blower Daniel Ellsberg ('We weren't on the wrong side. We are the wrong side.') and Walt Rostow, former National Security Advisor to Presidents Kennedy and Johnson, who saw Vietnam as: 'The price you pay for freedom ... it's the kind of risk you take to preserve the ideals we have.' Indirectly pitting Ellsberg, a symbol of transparent governance, against Rostow's domino-theory paranoiac, Davis makes no attempt at objectivity. He goes further towards the end of the film, juxtaposing comments by General Westmoreland – operations commander between 1964 and 1968 – about the lower value of life among Vietnamese people, with footage of a grief-stricken old woman throwing herself into her grandson's grave. However, Davis does show compassion for the regular and conscripted US soldiers who served and the parents of those killed, no matter their beliefs.

Hearts and Minds attracted criticism from both sides of the debate. Those supporting US involvement attacked the lack of focus on the Viet Cong's war crimes, while some anti-war campaigners felt the film should have gone further. Nevertheless, it played a pivotal role via its impact on domestic US audiences and offered a template for future documentaries, particularly in the aftermath of the 2003 invasion of Iraq.

IT'S A NON-FICTION FILM THAT IS

AN INQUIRY INTO MOTIVATION AND

ACTIONS AND ETHICS AND RESULTS.

Peter Davis

SHOAH

CLAUDE LANZMANN;
FRANCE/UK; 1985; 566 MINS

ALSO SEE

Night and Fog
(p.212)

Death Mills
(Billy Wilder, Hanuš Burger; 1945)
An early film detailing what Allied forces
found when they liberated the Nazi
extermination camps.

The Last of the Unjust
(Claude Lanzmann; 2013)
Lanzmann interviews the controversial
last president of the Jewish Council in
Czechoslovakia's Theresienstadt ghetto.

Babi Yar. Context
(Sergei Loznitsa; 2021)
Archive footage is assembled to detail
the Nazi massacre of over 33,000 Jews
on the outskirts of Kiev in 1941.

Editing more than 350 hours of interviews into a probing, frequently harrowing 566-minute witness documentary, Claude Lanzmann created one of the defining cinematic statements on the Holocaust. Eschewing archive footage in favour of first-person testimony, *Shoah* – the Hebrew translation for 'holocaust' – is the centrepiece of Lanzmann's decades-long documenting of the Nazi genocide.

A member of the French Resistance during the Second World War, who later became a journalist and academic, Lanzmann was commissioned by Israeli officials to make a two-hour film focusing on the stories of Jewish survivors. The plan was to deliver the completed version within 18 months. But the deeper Lanzmann immersed himself in the history of the Holocaust, the more expansive the project became. Funding was withdrawn, but Lanzmann continued. Over the next six years he recorded interviews with survivors, witnesses and perpetrators. Financing the project was difficult, locating some interviewees proved arduous and Lanzmann was threatened and even attacked – once being hospitalized for a month – as well as facing official attempts to obstruct his filming. *Shoah* then took a further five years to edit. Some interviews were intercut with contemporary footage from the site of a specific death camp, cementing the link between what happened and where it took place. (In two of the film's most memorable sequences, an engineer operates the same train he took people to their deaths in, while a barber from one of the camps talks about his experiences as he cuts someone's hair.)

The film's four areas of focus are the Warsaw Ghetto, the death camps at Treblinka and Auschwitz-Birkenau, and the Chełmno extermination camp. Lanzmann's decision to only feature first-hand testimonies adds immeasurably to the film's power and he was meticulous in the way interviews were recorded, transcribed and catalogued. (The English translations are held at the US Holocaust Museum in Washington, while the out-takes have formed the basis of five subsequent films produced by Lanzmann between 1997 and 2018.)

There were critics, particularly those who objected to the emphasis on Poland; some claimed that *Shoah* is too damning of the role played by the country and its people, while others stated it did not go far enough in detailing their culpability. But the film now stands as an essential document of what took place, and is the foundation of a wider body of work recording and memorializing the Holocaust.

MAKING A HISTORY WAS NOT WHAT I WANTED TO DO.

I WANTED TO CONSTRUCT SOMETHING MORE POWERFUL THAN THAT.

THE EMPEROR'S NAKED ARMY MARCHES ON

YUKI YUKITE, SHINGUN
KAZUO HARA;
JAPAN; 1987; 122 MINS

ALSO SEE

Burden of Dreams
(p.100)

Summer in Narita
(Shinsuke Ogawa; 1968)
A record of the farmers and students'
attempts to oppose the construction of
the Narita International Airport.

Extreme Private Eros: Love Song 1974
(Kazuo Hara; 1974)
Hara's unsettlingly documentary about
his ex-wife is also a frank portrait of
the filmmaker's obsessions.

Thus a Noise Speaks
(Kaori Oda; 2010)
The director restages the moment
she came out to her family, who
recreate their roles for camera.

For a filmmaker drawn to unconventional figures in Japanese society, Kazuo Hara found his perfect subject in Kenzō Okuzaki. A former member of the Japanese Imperial Army who was stationed in New Guinea during the Second World War, Okuzaki embarks on an investigation to uncover the truth behind two military executions during the Pacific campaign. Hara's startling film is a provocative character study that questions the notion of an objective cinema.

The Emperor's Naked Army Marches On follows Okuzaki as he travels around Japan in a van emblazoned with derisory slogans about Emperor Hirohito, whom he holds responsible for the horrors of the war. He visits members of his former regiment in an attempt to uncover the reason for the executions of the two men, who he subsequently discovers were killed after Japan had surrendered, making those responsible murderers. It becomes apparent that the executed men had been found guilty of cannibalism, but this revelation sits alongside other stories of what all the soldiers had to endure.

Okuzaki visits his targets early in the morning, hoping to catch them off guard. He is initially polite, but if he suspects he is being lied to he becomes violent, with one interviewee having to be taken to hospital. Okuzaki also employs subterfuge, using actors to play the parents of the dead soldiers in order to emotionally blackmail witnesses. All the while, Hara's camera keeps Okuzaki close, the investigation secondary to the filmmaker's fascination with his deeply conflicted subject.

The film opens with details of Okuzaki's past. He had been convicted three times, for murder, firing pachinko balls at the emperor and distributing pornographic caricatures featuring Hirohito. At the end of the film, he is jailed once again, sentenced to 12 years' hard labour, for attempting to murder the son of the former officer who ordered the executions. But Hara never judges his subject. Some critics have suggested he is too complicit in Okuzaki's actions. Nevertheless, the convergence of an uncompromising, anti-authoritarian filmmaker with an unruly subject hell-bent on challenging the 'polite' conservatism of Japanese society results in an incendiary film that defies any easy reading.

LESSONS OF DARKNESS

WERNER HERZOG;
FRANCE/UK/GERMANY;
1992; 54 MINS

ALSO SEE

Leviathan
(p.178)

Fata Morgana
(Werner Herzog; 1971)
Herzog's vision of the Sahara shifts
from a sense of awe at nature to a
record of mankind's abuse of it.

Junktopia
**(Chris Marker, John Chapman,
Frank Simeone; 1981)**
Artists have created a world of
human detritus, culled from the
ocean, in Emeryville, on the
outskirts of San Francisco.

*Petropolis: Aerial Perspectives
on the Alberta Tar Sands*
(Peter Mettler; 2009)
A striking visual essay on the impact
of the oil industry on the vast
tar sands in Canada.

Werner Herzog's otherworldly portrait of Kuwait following Iraq's 1990 invasion and subsequent scorched-earth retreat, which saw hundreds of oil wells set ablaze, is an expressionistic rumination on our propensity for destruction. A striking visual essay set to classical music, *Lessons of Darkness* – whose title is taken from a composition by François Couperin – was initially criticized for its lack of specificity. But the filmmaker saw something deeper in the burning oilfields and the suffering of a people: 'I set out to record crimes perpetrated against not just humanity, but Creation itself.'

Initially intending to make a film about famed US oil well firefighter Red Adair, Herzog instead became fascinated by the more rudimentary tactics employed by an international team battling the furnaces. Unfolding over 13 chapters, the film opens with Herzog's voiceover suggesting that the burning deserts are akin to an alien world: 'A planet in our solar system. White mountain ranges, clouds, a land shrouded in mist.' His words are spoken as plumes of smoke and the haze of fire obscure the landscape. The film then moves through two brief passages: 'A Capital City' and 'The War'; aerial shots of Kuwait City before the Iraqi invasion, and a handful of long shots showing the attack through night-vision optics. Aside from two additional passages, one detailing the instruments used in torture – tracking shots across tables with the tools laid out on them – and another featuring a woman whose husband was tortured and killed in front of her and their child, who has not spoken since, the film details the impact of the conflict on the landscape. Alongside the burning oilfields is the devastation left in the wake of a retreating army – destroyed vehicles, factories and buildings, all cloaked in ash and sand, like the remnants of a disappeared civilization. In one sequence, what appears to be a lustrous oasis is revealed to be a once verdant landscape now drowning in oil, with all life slowly being suffocated by it.

Lessons of Darkness sits alongside two other striking visual essays by the filmmaker: the eerie *Fata Morgana* (1971) and semi-fictional *The Wild Blue Yonder* (2005). Each features a narrator who might be from another world, commenting on the wonder and calamity of human achievement. But here, Herzog's vision is at its most bleak. The extraordinary work of the firefighters notwithstanding, *Lessons of Darkness* leaves us in no doubt about humanity's ruinous tendencies.

THE POWER OF NIGHTMARES

ADAM CURTIS;
UK; 2004; 157 MINS

ALSO SEE

LBJ
(p.213)

The Secret Rulers of the World
(Jon Ronson; 2001)
The British investigative journalist enters
the world of conspiracy theorists.

Bitter Lake
(Adam Curtis; 2015)
An intensive account of the historical
relationship between the US and
Saudi Arabia, and its subsequent
impact on the Middle East.

Reason
(Anand Patwardhan; 2018)
Over eight chapters, Patwardhan's
expansive and critical film assesses
the impact of Hindu majoritarianism.

According to Adam Curtis' persuasive and unsettling three-part documentary, the events of 11 September 2001 brought to a head two ideologies that had been fermenting for decades. Although they appeared diametrically opposed, Curtis argues that Islamic Fundamentalism and Neoconservatism drew from the same cultural well. And their resulting dominance on the world stage introduced an era that the writer-director describes in the series' subtitle as 'The Rise of the Politics of Fear'.

Curtis' compelling three-part series traces the attacks of 9/11 and subsequent events back to the 1950s and the intellectual inquiries of two men: Sayyid Qutb and Leo Strauss. Egyptian-born Qutb taught for two years in the US and saw a moral decadence that he believed would be the West's undoing. Likewise, Strauss was a philosopher at the University of Chicago and was convinced that the US required a morally-driven ideological foundation to survive. Qutb would be executed for his beliefs back in Egypt, but his writings became the bedrock of the Egyptian Muslim Brotherhood and would eventually inform the radical beliefs of al-Qaeda. Strauss would also attract acolytes – including Paul Wolfowitz and Donald Rumsfeld – who subscribed to his ideology and would eventually preside over US political life. Both views held that fear, not aspiration, would sustain the society they envisaged, even if the enemy they identified was overstated or mostly fictitious.

The Power of Nightmares was Curtis' most high-profile series to date and perfectly exemplifies his approach to filmmaking. He joined the BBC in the 1980s and soon developed a style that employed a complex montage of archive and library images, accompanied by his calm, unruffled narration and an eclectic soundtrack. A polemicist, his work has attracted as many critics as it has admirers. This series argues that the invasion of Afghanistan put an end to whatever international influence al-Qaeda had. However, the Neoconservatives' need to create an outsized enemy resulted in the promotion of an exaggerated network of radicalized troops to engage in a 'War on Terror'.

In an age when the concept of fake news has shifted from a periphery of marginalized conspiracy theorists to the mainstream media, and distrust of governments and tech giants is metastasizing, Curtis' body of work, from his earliest documentary shorts through to his sprawling six-part series *Can't Get You Out of My Head* (2021), suggests that confusion is exactly what certain ideologically minded politicians have been seeking. However, he concludes that a politically expedient way of controlling society has unwittingly transformed into a Pandora's box that is now out of control.

THE WAR

Within days of the 2001 terrorist assault on the World Trade Center towers, images of the attack were circling the world. They were followed by documentaries detailing that day's events, from on-the-ground records such as *9/11* (2002) to conspiracy-driven accounts like *Loose Change* (2005–09). However, it was the subsequent War on Terror that saw the number of documentaries being made about these tensions dramatically increase.

International journalists and filmmakers were frequently embedded with troops. The films they produced were visceral but also opened the debate on how much the media – from news journalists to independent filmmakers – were being controlled by official bodies such as the military. However, there is little doubting the power of films such as Sebastian Junger and Tim Heatherington's *Restrepo* or Janus Metz's *Armadillo* (both 2010). Questions regarding the freedom of the press are tackled in Jehane Noujaim's *Control Room* (2004), which detailed the US establishment's uneasy relationship with Arabic news agency Al Jazeera.

The way the media manipulates and is manipulated has long been a fascination for Adam Curtis. If his

144

The Power of Nightmares (2004, p.142) challenged conventional wisdom regarding the narrative behind the War on Terror, his subsequent film *Bitter Lake* (2015) offered up an alternate recent history of the Middle East and Gulf region.

Charles Ferguson's *No End in Sight* (2007) gave a critical overview of the first three years of the US occupation of Iraq. But it was the collection of films that focused on human rights abuses that crystalized the strong sentiment against the prolonged occupation enacted under the guise of regime change. Alex Gibney's *Taxi to the Dark Side* (2007) and Errol Morris' *Standard Operating Procedure* (2008) became the key films in confronting torture and human rights abuses, while Eugene Jarecki's *Why We Fight* (2005) explored the role of business in the arena of global conflict. And Michael Moore's *Fahrenheit 9/11* (2004), which presented a scathing critique of the Bush administration, attracted almost universal critical praise and became a rare documentary blockbuster hit.

Opposite: *Fahrenheit 9/11* (2002)
Above: *Taxi to the Dark Side* (2007)

ON TERROR

WALTZ WITH BASHIR

VALZ IM BASHIR
ARI FOLMAN; ISRAEL/FRANCE/
GERMANY/US/FINLAND/
SWITZERLAND/BELGIUM/
AUSTRALIA; 2008; 90 MINS

ALSO SEE

El Sopar
(p.60)

Massacre
(Monika Borgmann, Lokman Slim,
Hermannn Theissen; 2005)
Six unidentified individuals
discuss their roles in the Sabra
and Shatila massacre.

Tower
(Keith Maitland; 2016)
The 1966 University of Texas tower
shootings are reconstructed through
rotoscope animation.

Flee
(Jonas Poher Rasmussen; 2021)
An animated account of a young
man's journey to escape political,
cultural and sexual persecution.

Ari Folman's vivid exploration of events that that led up to the infamous Sabra and Shatila massacre in Lebanon is constructed as an investigation into memory. The filmmaker employs a variety of animation techniques, before turning to live-action archive footage for his powerful dénouement.

A black hole in the memory of the filmmaker, a former Israeli Defence Force conscript, Folman's time in the armed forces is gradually reconstructed as he attempts to reconcile the role he played in the 1982 massacre carried out against Palestinian and Lebanese Shiites by Christian Phalangist forces. His journey begins with a friend regaling a dream in which a pack of wild dogs rampages through city streets until they reach the entrance to his apartment block. The friend believes they're a symbol of the animals he killed – watchdogs in small villages – as he and fellow IDF members hunted down PLO members. The dream prompts Folman to ruminate on his own experiences and to realize how little he can recall.

Through his visits to friends and former colleagues, Folman pieces together life in the army. While acknowledging the fear felt by the conscripts, as well as the extreme situations they found themselves in, Folman also highlights the callousness of young men engaged in a conflict they are utterly unprepared for. Intermingling knockabout humour with increasingly surreal sequences (accentuated by Max Richter's atmospheric score and a rich catalogue of hits from the era), Folman reveals how his memory of the past has been constructed through a combination of fragmented recollections and fevered dreams. But as the narrative shifts towards the events at

Sabra and Shatila, and Folman's memory of his role in them returns, the film eschews ambiguity for a stark and sombre tone.

Animation director Yoni Goodman's innovative combination of different styles – computer-generated, hand-drawn and cut-out – add immeasurably to the film's surreal tone. And alongside his friends and fellow former conscripts, Folman interviews a high-ranking officer, a renowned Israeli broadcast journalist and a professor who specializes in psychological trauma. These testimonies take *Waltz with Bashir* beyond the reconstruction an individual's forgotten past, daring to confront a nation's 'collective amnesia' over its involvement in an atrocity.

FIVE BROKEN CAMERAS

EMAD BURNAT, GUY DAVIDI;
OCCUPIED PALESTINIAN
TERRITORY/ISRAEL/FRANCE/
NETHERLANDS; 2011; 94 MINS

Emad Burnat's filmed diary finds him more an activist than observer, highlighting in stark terms what it means to be oppressed. It is a moving account of events that took place over five years, when Israeli settlers began to occupy the land belonging to the village of Bil'in. It lies some seven miles west of Ramallah, in Palestine's central West Bank, and is the filmmaker's home.

Burnat begins his film in 2005, recording home life following the birth of his son Gibreel. But he soon turns his camera on the actions of Israeli armed forces and settlers, who become a constant presence in and around the village. Over the next five years, his cameras are destroyed by bullets, gas grenades and physical attacks, as he witnesses his brothers being shot and arrested, the deaths of friends, olive orchards set on fire and attempts by settlers to take land by force. He also records celebrations over legal victories, brief moments of respite with his family and the continual resilience of an embattled community.

Five Broken Cameras offers no overarching analysis of the Israeli-Palestinian conflict beyond the events that impact Burnat and his community. (There is a record of violence that erupted in a neighbouring town, but it does little more than highlight how Bil'in's predicament is far from solitary.) Israeli filmmaker Davidi's involvement is less to present a balanced perspective than it is an act of solidarity by a filmmaker who visited Bil'in and was so shocked by what he saw that he offered to help Burnat edit his years of footage into a cogent record. The film details the building of a wall separating land that had been in the village's possession for centuries and is unflinching in highlighting unprovoked attacks by the Israeli army. (Some of the footage from these sequences was shot by other camera operators who are recognized in the film's credits.) Victories are few, and whatever progress the village makes is unlikely to change its situation with the settlers. Ultimately, Burnat's film is a tribute to his community; those arrested, those who died in the struggle and those who continue to fight peacefully for their homes.

Emad Burnat

MANY PEOPLE COME TO MAKE FILMS ABOUT OUR SITUATION, BUT THEY DON'T KNOW THE REALITY OF OUR LIFE.

I THINK ART CAN CHANGE THE CONVERSATION . . .

YOU CAN'T HAVE ACTIVISM AROUND A PROBLEM NO ONE ACKNOWLEDGES.

Joshua Oppenheimer

THE ACT OF KILLING

LEKTIONEN IN FINSTERNIS
JOSHUA OPPENHEIMER;
UK/DENMARK/NORWAY;
2012; 117 MINS

How can a film grapple with an unresolved history of genocide in a country where its perpetrators live without fear of conviction or reprisal? Joshua Oppenheimer invited key participants from Indonesia's bloody recent past to recreate their acts in the style of their favourite movie genres. The result is, by turns, revealing, shocking and, for one of its participants, revelatory.

In 1965, a coup failed to depose President Sukarno of Indonesia. Subsequent reprisals put Army General Suharto at the head of the 'New Order' dictatorship, which oversaw the torture and execution of Communists or anyone opposed to the new regime. Within a year, members of a nascent right-wing paramilitary movement, deputized thugs and street gangsters were responsible for the deaths of at least half a million people. Among the most notorious killers were Anwar Congo and Adi Zulkadry, who take centre stage in Oppenheimer's film.

These men, along with other conspirators from the era, including business leaders and the editor of a national newspaper, talk openly about their actions. In one sequence, Congo shows how he made killing more effective and with as little blood shed as possible. Oppenheimer offers no wider context to these killings – no history of the events following Suharto's taking power. Instead, his focus lies with the actions of individuals and their feelings about what they did; the conversations between Congo and Zulkadry as they are made up for one of their films are horrifically frank.

It is during this sequence that a neighbour of Congo's, who is working on the film-within-a-film, talks nervously about the abduction and murder of his stepfather. Oppenheimer highlights that former victims and their families appear more fearful of speaking out than the killers. (It's an idea more fully fleshed out in the filmmaker's companion film *The Look of Silence*, 2014.) However, in this instance Zulkadry responds, 'I'm absolutely aware that we were cruel'. Late in the film, Congo also faces up to his crimes. He revisits the place where he killed many of his victims. His body convulses at the thought of what he did. It's little compensation for the many victims, but his participation in Oppenheimer's strange and unsettling film at least forced him to face up to his crimes, if only for a moment.

STATE FUNERAL

SERGEI LOZNITSA;
NETHERLANDS/LITHUANIA;
2019; 135 MINS

In the immediate aftermath of Joseph Stalin's death, the vice-like grip he once held over the Soviet Union continued to inspire terror and subservience. The Congress of the Communist Party of the Soviet Union planned a monumental film of his funeral. It's the footage from that abandoned project that Sergei Loznitsa has reconstructed in his portrait of a society's outpouring of grief; not because it was felt, but because it was demanded.

Loznitsa wisely avoids analysis of either Stalin's rule or the events that took place in the wake of his death. There are no talking heads or voiceover commentaries, just footage – both black-and-white and colour, and often strikingly beautiful – documenting a nation in a state of mourning. It opens at various locations around the USSR, from Moscow to satellite states, with radio announcements broadcasting news of the leader's death. Like the eulogies heard later by party apparatchiks, obsequiousness was the order of the day. By contrast, the expressions on the populace are, for the most part, difficult to read. There are some tears, but more common are stony grimaces – a default expression that might have been perfected through decades of Stalin's rule.

Reactions are mostly the same among the masses who turn out to pay their respects, or catch a glimpse of the dead leader, as he lies in state. More than any other sequence in the film, it's here that the colour footage creates a profound sense of unease. Many of those shuffling past the body will have likely suffered some indignity at the hands, or on the orders, of the dead leader, but here he lies, atop a bed of palm leaves and flowers – an obscene monument.

State Funeral is one chapter in Loznitsa's series of impressively constructed archival documentaries, which re-examine moments in Soviet and Eastern Bloc history. In the film's end credits Loznitsa tells us that Joseph Stalin was responsible for the death, imprisonment or starvation of more than 42 million people. Within three years of his death on 5 March 1953, a policy of de-Stalinization swept across the USSR. His body was eventually disinterred from Lenin's Tomb and buried at the Kremlin Wall. His fall from grace – more recent attempts to rewrite his legacy notwithstanding – may have been swift, but Loznitsa's fascinating archive document highlights how pervasive his control over the Soviet Union was.

WHEN YOU FIND A TREASURE TROVE LIKE THIS, YOU NEVER ASK WHAT MOTIVATES YOU TO WORK WITH IT.

Sergei Loznitsa

I FOUND SOME TREASURE! THAT IS THE MOTIVATION.

FOR SAMA

WAAD AL-KATEAB, EDWARD WATTS;
UK/SYRIA/US; 2019; 100 MINS

A rumination on life during a bloody and brutal conflict, *For Sama* is a cinematic letter from Waad Al-Kateab to her daughter, a harrowing account of the tragedy that unfolded in Syria and a record of the people who gave their lives in the fight for democracy. In both its intimacy and immediacy, the film underpins how technology has enabled us to record daily life, under any circumstances.

Over the last two decades, the increased quality and widespread availability of digital cameras has transformed the role of citizen journalists around the world. From Buddhist monks railing against state coercion in Burma to the rising tide of activism that became Occupy Wall Street, activists have transformed into on-the-ground chroniclers of our rapidly changing times. This urgency reached new heights with the revolutionary tide that swept the Arab world.

A few months after the Arab Spring began in Tunisia in December 2010, anti-government demonstrations broke out in Syria. The refusal of Bashar al-Assad to concede to reformers' demands resulted in a drawn-out civil war. A key battleground was Aleppo, which university student Al-Kateab had made her home. She began filming as students took to the streets and continued to document events for five years, becoming a journalist for Channel 4 News in the UK. She also captured footage of life as it unfolded around her: of her friends, life in the hospitals she worked in, the burgeoning relationship with one of the doctors who chose to remain in the city, their wedding and the subsequent birth of their daughter, Sama. Shifting back and forth over five years, capturing the horror of the Russian-supported Syrian army assaults, along with the family's eventual – and narrow – escape, Al-Kateab records for her daughter the sacrifices so many people made for the right to live in a democracy. Harrowing moments are leavened by the humanity of the medics and staff in a makeshift hospital – the only aid available to the remaining civilian population.

Deeply personal, yet socially and politically potent in grappling with what took place across the country, *For Sama* presents a ground-up account of the cost of the conflict. As Al-Kateab notes, it is her attempt to comprehend what took place, but also a record for her daughter to understand the lives her parents lived. It might also imbue in her the hope that she will one day return in peace to the land her family once called home.

IT'S NOT JUST A FILM

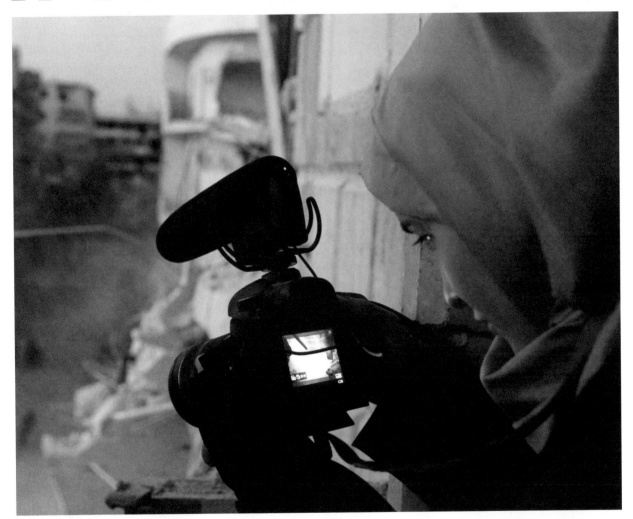

IT'S MY LIFE.

Waad Al-Kateab

EXTERMINATE ALL THE BRUTES

RAOUL PECK;
US; 2021; 232 MINS

ALSO SEE

I Am Not Your Negro
(p.84)

*C.S.A.: The Confederate
States of America*
(Kevin Wilmott; 2004)
A documentary within a documentary
that imagines the North lost the
US Civil War.

Concerning Violence
(Göran Olsson; 2014)
An account of the struggles against
colonial rule, inspired by Franz Fanon's
1961 text *The Wretched of the Earth*.

African Apocalypse
(Rob Lemkin; 2020)
British-Nigerian poet Femi Nylander
details the generational impact of
French Colonial rule in Africa.

Raoul Peck's ambitious serial documentary opens with a challenge to certain accepted Western historical narratives. 'Three words that summarize the whole of humanity,' Peck's voiceover informs us. 'Civilization. Colonialization. Extermination. These words run forcibly through Western world history. The same way they run to the core of US history.' The statement lays out the strategy Peck employs across the series, shifting between historical events in the US and wider world.

Continuing an examination of racial prejudice and colonialism that has defined much of Peck's work, *Exterminate All the Brutes* is an unflinching account of the lives of those who have been on the receiving end of 'progress', during five centuries of conquest, exploitation and subjugation. Three texts are vital to Peck's thesis: Sven Lindqvist's *Exterminate All the Brutes* (1996), Roxanne Dunbar-Ortiz's *An Indigenous Peoples' History of the United States* (2014) and Michel-Rolph Trouillot's *Silencing the Past* (1995). Between them, these studies chart Europe's genocidal control of Africa, a history of the first people in the US and an overview of the use and abuse of power in Haiti.

Beginning with the Spanish Inquisition, when the notion of biological race was first conceived, Peck moves through the expeditions of Columbus, the transatlantic slave trade, European governments' colonial power grabs, the rise of the Nazis, Hiroshima and its after-effects, and more recent political events. The series employs a barrage of images to flesh out its case, from charts, illustrations, texts and animation, to photographs, narrative and archive film footage, and dramatic recreation. The latter, used sparingly, features Josh Hartnett as a variety of characters from history, but together representing an archetype of the colonial agressor.

Peck brings his own family's story into the mix, grounding the larger narrative arc of history within a moving personal context. And as with his previous *I Am Not Your Negro* (2016, p.84), the past informs the present. Just as that film interwove racism in the US throughout the twentieth century with the rise of populism, Donald Trump, white supremacy and Black Lives Matter, in *Exterminate All the Brutes* Peck shines a light on some of the cruellest moments of human history, not to highlight the barbarity of the past, but to make clear how the constructs that enabled these atrocities are still present in our world.

SCIENCE

& NATURE

NANOOK OF THE NORTH

ROBERT FLAHERTY; US/FRANCE;
1922; 78 MINS

ALSO SEE

Land Without Bread
(p.210)

Grass: A Nation's Battle for Life
(Merian C. Cooper,
Ernest B. Schoedsack; 1925)
A chronicle of Persian tribesmen in
search of arable land for their livestock.

Profils paysans
(Raymond Depardon; 2001–08)
A trilogy by the acclaimed photographer
and filmmaker, focusing on farm
life in southern France.

Faya Dayi
(Jessica Beshir; 2021)
An atmospheric portrait of the role
played by the psychoactive plant
khat within Ethopian culture.

Robert Flaherty's ground-breaking portrait of an Inuk family eking out an existence in the Canadian Arctic proved successful with international audiences. One of the earliest films to combine non-fiction and narrative cinema, it would become a key work in the debate over what constitutes a documentary. It is also seen as an early example of 'salvage ethnography', a film that recorded a way of life that no longer exists.

Flaherty's career as a filmmaker came about by chance. He was prospector searching for mineral deposits along the Hudson Bay when his employer suggested that he take a camera to record his experiences. However, most of the thousands of feet he recorded on his early trips were destroyed in a fire. Flaherty then spent four years attempting to raise money for his film, which eventually changed from a general travelogue to a more detailed examination of one family's life on the coldest reaches of the Earth. A French fur company eventually funded the project, which was shot over the course of one year, starting in August 1920.

Flaherty's principal focus was Allakariallak, a hunter in the Itivimuit tribe, whom he renamed Nanook for the film. With a crew mostly comprised of locals – who reportedly became more proficient with the equipment than their employer – Flaherty filmed daily life, from hunting and fishing to building igloos and surviving on the icy tundra. The harshness of the environment made even the most rudimentary filming difficult, with everything having to be shot using natural light. The challenge of shooting inside an igloo was resolved by the construction of an open-ended ice home, which nevertheless conveyed what living conditions were like for its inhabitants. When it came to hunting, the Inuit involved in the film had long favoured guns to spears. However, Flaherty encouraged Allakariallak to employ more traditional weapons on camera, as witnessed in the sequence where Nanook and his fellow hunters capture and kill a walrus.

Factual accuracy was secondary to the pursuit of dramatic impact. The film even ends by informing us that Nanook died two years later from starvation, when Allakariallak actually succumbed to tuberculosis. But the resilience and invention of a people living in the harshest conditions nonetheless shines through. And Flaherty's film remains a landmark – albeit one whose blurring of the line between fact and fabrication remains controversial – in the history of documentary cinema.

NANOOK IS ONE OF THE MOST VITAL AND UNFORGETTABLE HUMAN BEINGS EVER RECORDED ON FILM.

Film critic Roger Ebert

LIFE ON EARTH

DAVID ATTENBOROUGH
(CONCEIVED, WRITTEN,
PRESENTED); UK; 1979;
715 MINS

ALSO SEE

Cow
(p.179)

Planet Earth
(Conceived by David
Attenborough; 2006)
An awe-inspiring record, employing
state-of-the-art technology, capturing
life around the globe.

Encounters at the End of the World
(Werner Herzog; 2008)
A portrait of human and animal life
in and around the McMurdo Station
in Antarctica.

Jane
(Brett Morgen; 2017)
An unvarnished portrait of primatologist
Jane Goodall and her life in Africa.

The availability of increasingly mobile technology transformed natural history filmmaking and made *Life on Earth* possible. The template for future documentary studies of the natural world, it was conceived, written and presented by a figure who would become synonymous with the form: David Attenborough.

Life on Earth is a 13-part series of 55-minute films that trace the evolution of life on our planet. In the first episode alone, Attenborough takes us from a South American rainforest and the Galápagos Islands, via the Grand Canyon and Yellowstone Park in the US, to Lake Superior in Canada and the Flinders Ranges in Australia, to reveal evidence of the earliest forms of life. From there, he traces evolutionary development; from insects to plant life; the journey of creatures from sea to land and into the air; how mammals developed; the complexity of food chains, from herbivores to predators; and the ascent of humankind. With his warm, clipped tones – a voice that would become one of the most trusted in broadcasting – Attenborough proved himself a passionate and compelling guide. He imparted a wealth of knowledge with a sense of wonder as infectious as it proved seemingly limitless. Nowhere is this more evident than in his very close encounter with a group of mountain gorillas in Rwanda. On his second day among them, the female and two infants began to groom him. He described it as 'one of the most exciting encounters of my life'.

Attenborough had been making nature programmes for the BBC since 1954, initially with his television series *Zoo Quest* (1954–64). *Life on Earth* came about after an influential decade heading up BBC2. The series took three years to complete and employed a variety of innovative filming techniques, such as filming a bat in slow motion in a wind tunnel. By the end of the shoot, the crew had travelled 1.5 million miles. Combined with Attenborough's detailed narration and Edward Williams' celebrated experimental score, *Life on Earth* revealed the world as never before to a global audience. Attenborough would continue to build on the series' success with subsequent forays into the natural world, making the most of increasingly sophisticated technology. But through its intelligence, passion and Attenborough's physical presence throughout, *Life on Earth* remains the documentary landmark by which all other natural history programmes should be judged.

COSMOS

VARIOUS; US/UK;
1980; 780 MINS

What *Life on Earth* (1979, p.162) was to documenting the natural world, *Cosmos* became to the expanding universe. The most successful science programme ever made, watched by over 500 million people across 60 countries, *Cosmos* made its host, academic and Pulitzer Prize-winning cosmologist Carl Sagan, a household name. And it reignited a fascination with astronomy that had been absent since the heyday of NASA's lunar missions.

Episode one, 'The Shores of the Cosmic Ocean', opens with Sagan overlooking a turbulent sea, informing us that: 'The cosmos is all that is, ever was or ever will be.' He boards a 'ship of the imagination', a fantastic interstellar craft shaped like a dandelion seed, which transports him into space, accompanied by Vangelis' ethereal score. Standing on its bridge, Sagan journeys through galaxies, across time and around the Earth, his narratives seamlessly combining history, myths and belief systems with facts about the known universe.

Like the earlier landmark television series *Civilisation* (1969) and *The Ascent of Man* (1973), *Cosmos* was a hugely ambitious authored documentary – the series was co-written by Sagan with Ann Druyan and Steven Soter – that balanced grand narratives with more intimate storytelling. The Japanese samurai myth regarding the Heike crab is the starting point for a discussion of artificial and natural selection, evolution and the discovery of DNA. The planet Mars is pictured through the prism of nineteenth-century science fiction, alongside more recent scientific research. The beliefs of various societies and the theories of early scientists are contextualized within a constantly expanding knowledge of the universe. And Sagan talks with young students in a Brooklyn classroom about the myths and nature of stars and constellations. With his commanding but softly spoken voice, Sagan exudes a sage-like screen presence.

The series was shot on a combination of video and film. It made extensive use of available special and visual effects technology, allowing its presenter to walk among the stars. But it's Sagan's passion and openness – taking delight in what we know and exuding a fathomless curiosity about the countless things we don't – that makes *Cosmos* such a riveting journey.

THE UNIVERSE WILL ALWAYS BE MUCH RICHER

THAN OUR ABILITY TO UNDERSTAND IT.

Carl Sagan

165

KOYAANISQATSI

GODFREY REGGIO;
US; 1982; 86 MINS

A dialogue-free compendium of images, Godfrey Reggio's cinematic travelogue documents our presence on Earth. Employing a variety of in-camera effects and accompanied throughout by minimalist composer Philip Glass' hypnotic score, *Koyaanisqatsi* marvels at the beauty of our planet and ponders our impact upon it, highlighting our destructive tendencies.

Taking its title from the Hopi word for the phrase 'life out of balance', *Koyaanisqatsi* was conceived when Reggio and cinematographer Ron Fricke worked together on a media campaign in New Mexico. With funds remaining from their project, they decided to create a 'pure film', one whose narrative was gleaned solely from the juxtaposition of images. They subsequently travelled the country, recording environments that caught their attention. With more funding, they were able to incorporate time-lapse photography, which would eventually become a signature element of the film, alongside the use of slow motion and double exposure. As it neared completion, Francis Ford Coppola requested a screening. Impressed, he added his name to the credits, guaranteeing it greater publicity. The film was a modest success, but its reputation has grown with time.

Divided into chapters, *Koyaanisqatsi*'s pace works in tandem with Glass' arpeggio-driven combination of choral and orchestral compositions; undulating with the movement of clouds and oceans, or frenetic as it channels the velocity of urban life. Bookended by images of rock art from Horseshoe Canyon in Utah – inserted at the suggestion of Coppola – the film opens in an untouched natural world, with breathtakingly beautiful aerial shots of land and water, before an explosion marks human intervention. From there, the film shows humanity's dominance of the environment, often transforming it completely. The rural is replaced by the metropolitan and life moves ever faster, until the film's penultimate shot, of a rocket engine careering back towards the Earth's surface. Graceful yet haunting,this meachanical Icarus represents the hubris of our ambitions and achievements within the wider context of nature.

Koyaanisqatsi is the first in a trilogy of thematically linked films directed by Reggio. *Powaqqatsi* (1988) focused on life in developing countries, while *Naqoyqatsi* (2002) witnesses the shift from a natural to a digital world. Fricke would also embark on a career as a director, most notably with the sumptuously shot 70mm feature *Baraka* (1992). But none attain the cohesiveness or capture the shock of the new of Reggio's visually dazzling debut.

... I WANTED TO MAKE A FILM WHERE THE AUDIENCE COMPLETED THE SUBJECT.

Godfrey Reggio

FOR ALL MANKIND

AL REINERT; US; 1989;
80 MINS

ALSO SEE

Leviathan
(p.178)

State of Weightlessness
(Maciej J. Drygas; 1994)
An exploration of the psychological
and metaphysical impact of the
Soviet space programme.

In the Shadow of the Moon
(David Sington; 2007)
Previously unseen footage of the
NASA lunar landings is intercut with
reminiscences of the astronauts.

The Lebanese Rocket Society
(Joana Hadjithomas,
Khalil Joreige; 2012)
The history of a group of scientists who
developed rocket technology at the
height of the Cold War.

Bookended by excerpts from President John F. Kennedy's 1962 speech promoting NASA's lunar programme, Al Reinert's richly detailed documentary, the first to draw on the US space agency's expansive film archive, reconstructs the US space program as one single journey. Featuring voiceover testimonies by the astronauts and footage from the Gemini and Apollo missions, *For All Mankind* opens with the inferno of a rocket launch, journeys to the Moon and returns us to Earth.

There were a total of nine lunar missions between 1968 and 1972. Six of those saw twelve astronauts step onto the Moon's surface. The Apollo programme was, Reinert noted, 'the largest and most expensive undertaking in the history of man that wasn't devoted to war'. Reinert was rapt by the ambition of these NASA missions, which captured the imagination of the world. In 1976, he began interviewing former astronauts, eventually clocking up more than 80 hours of testimonies. It was while researching a magazine story about the lunar missions that he learned of NASA's vast repository of footage shot by the astronauts. Gaining approval to sift through it, Reinert and editor Susan Korda, aided by NASA editor Don Pickard – who had been assigned to the Apollo missions – spent the next decade working their way through six million feet of film. Producer, polymath and pioneer of ambient music, Brian Eno, was subsequently commissioned to score the film, his music accompanying the astronauts' voices.

Reinert used an optical printer to scan each 16mm frame of footage and blow it up to 35mm. The result is breathtaking. The crisp, formal beauty of the exterior shots, from the close-up of the rockets as they launch, through their journey into space and the various activities on the Moon, contrasts with the more casual footage recorded by the astronauts in the spacecraft. Eno's score – co-written with Daniel Lanois and Roger Eno – doesn't so much power the narrative along as drift with the imagery, by turns underscoring the starkness of the lunar landscape and emphasizing the warmth of the astronauts' interactions. The images recorded by these explorers were the first taken of our planet from space. Decades on, Reinert's assembly of them still inspires awe, but also reminds us of the precariousness of the Earth amid the vast chasm of space.

A FRAGILE

By the end of his career, Jacques Cousteau had become an ardent campaigner for the environment. As Liz Garbus details in her documentary *Becoming Cousteau* (2021), the programmes he made in the 1970s were a stark contrast to his and Louis Malle's 1956 Cannes winner *The Silent World*. They also went against the grain of what many people wanted to see or hear. Times have changed. David Attenborough's first landmark nature series *Life on Earth* (1979, p.162) didn't grapple with the footprint we were leaving on the world. But witnessing changes to the planet over the years shifted his position. And unlike Cousteau's audience, when Attenborough spoke, the world listened.

The environmental documentary has become one of the most significant genres in factual filmmaking over the course of the last two decades. The topics run the gamut, from the destructive impact of industries to the depletion of natural resources. Davis Guggenheim's *An Inconvenient Truth* (2006), featuring Al Gore's climate talk, became a rallying cry for environmentalism. But films had already been highlighting the dangers inherent in the way we were living. Godfrey Reggio's *Koyaanisqatsi* (1982, p.166) inspired a series of pictorial travelogues that highlighted our interaction with nature, while Jennifer Baichwal's portrait of

Above: *An Inconvenient Truth* (2006)
Opposite: *Blackfish* (2013)

Edward Burtynsky, *Manufactured Landscapes* (2006, p.173) took a more elliptical route in detailing the way we are transforming the world around us.

The campaigning documentary has proven particularly effective in focusing on the plight of animals, from dolphins (*The Cove*, 2009) and orcas (*Blackfish*, 2013) to gorillas (*Virunga*, 2014) and bees (*Honeyland*, 2019). Other films veered towards a more expansive worldview, whether they focused on the potential loss of fresh water (*Blue Gold: World Water Wars*, 2008) or the role of the business landscape in promulgating exploitation without responsibility (*The Corporation*, 2003). Then there were the films that defied any simple categorization, from the science fiction-themed doomsday tone of *Age of Stupid* (2009) to grappling with the lifespan of nuclear waste and how to communicate its dangers to a population in the distant future (*Into Eternity*, 2010, p.174).

WORLD

GRIZZLY MAN

WERNER HERZOG;
US; 2005; 103 MINS

Werner Herzog found his perfect subject in Timothy Treadwell. In 2003, the self-proclaimed saviour of Alaska's brown bear and his girlfriend Amie Huguenard were killed by one of the animals as they slept in their tent. Employing excerpts from the many hours of footage Treadwell shot over his final summers in Alaska, *Grizzly Man* pits one individual's idealistic worldview against the indifference of nature.

Treadwell spent 13 summers living among the bears in Katmai National Park. He used his experiences and the footage he shot to travel around US schools, highlighting his activities and celebrating the beauty of the animals he 'protected'. His fame increased with each year, as did the consternation of the park's authorities, who accused him of breaching regulations regarding contact with the wildlife. Treadwell's behaviour during his last summer became more erratic and, against the wishes of Huguenard, who was fearful of the bears, they remained in the park later than they normally would. Herzog shows the site of the attack and, in the film's most contentious scene, we see the reaction of a friend of Treadwell's as she watches Herzog listen to the audio recording of the fateful bear attack.

Herzog presents Treadwell as a Walter Mitty-esque figure who struggled to find a place in everyday society. The bears gave him a sense of meaning in the world, no matter how misguided it was. To Herzog, Treadwell was a trailblazer whose recordings gave his life import; not the footage Treadwell shot of his performing to camera, but what Herzog regards as 'ecstatic truth' – seemingly throwaway moments that offer wondrous examples of life in a wilderness, from reeds blowing in the wind to fox paws dancing on a tent canvas. Herzog's attraction to these moments corroborates cinematographer and frequent collaborator Ed Lachman's belief about the filmmaker's approach: 'What is strongest is the content of the images, not a formalistic attitude about what the image is.'

How Herzog edits Treadwell's footage with his own highlights two contrasting worldviews. *Grizzly Man* reinforces a wary regard for nature that Herzog has explored throughout much of his fiction and documentary work, including his subsequent *Encounters at the End of the World* (2007). Just as he found his polar opposite in Treadwell, Herzog saw in the bears Treadwell adored, 'the overwhelming indifference of nature'.

MANUFACTURED LANDSCAPES

JENNIFER BAICHWAL;
CANADA; 2006; 90 MINS

ALSO SEE

West of the Tracks
(p.72)

Up the Yangtze
(Yung Chang; 2007)
Employees on a cruise ship witness the changes brought about by the Three Gorges Dam.

Waste Land
(Lucy Walker, Karen Harley, João Jardim; 2010)
An artist creates portraits of people working on the world's largest landfill, outside Rio de Janeiro.

Welcome to Sodom
(Christian Krönes, Florian Weigensamer; 2018)
An account of life for workers eking out a living on one of the world's largest technology dumps, in Accra, Ghana.

Jennifer Baichwal accompanied Edward Burtynsky on a journey through China's industrial society, aiming to record the photographer at work. What she achieved expands far beyond the frame of her subject's images, capturing the vastness of the country's colossal commercial activity, the cost to its workers and witnessing in real-time the transformation of entire landscapes.

Burtynsky's work encompasses globalization, industrialization, environmentalism and politics. He travelled to China to record 'the industrial landscape as a way of defining who we are and our relationship to the planet'. These words are spoken by Burtynsky as Baichwal's camera moves, in an eight-minute opening tracking shot, along the length of an immense factory floor, taking in the workers as they toil at their stations. It ends by zooming out on Burtynsky's beautifully composed shot of this environment. But a more telling moment happens in Baichwal's next shot. A bell rings and workers leave their stations, save for one lone worker, who is fast asleep. Likewise, in Burtynsky's next set-up, workers in clothes whose colours match the factory units they come from appear aligned in a formation that resembles a dayglo take on George Orwell's *1984*. Again, the image produced is both awe-inspiring and unsettling. But Baichwal's capturing workers being reprimanded by their manager adds emphasis to the human drama of this sequence.

Burtynsky documents how the landscape of the world has changed. He and Baichwal continued their collaboration on *Watermark* (2013) and *Anthropocene: The Human Epoch* (2019), which focus on, respectively, humanity's use and abuse of water systems, and the transformative role we have played in reshaping the whole planet. Of the three, *Manufactured Landscapes* focuses as much on Burtynsky's process as his subject.

From a factory floor to a shipbreaking beach in Bangladesh, and demolished cities on the brink of submersion beneath a vast man-made lake as part of China's Three Gorges Dam project, Baichwal's film successfully conveys the spirit of Burtynsky's work, but is no less breathtaking in capturing its own images of immense scale. However, it is moments of intimacy – capturing snatches of conversation or witnessing people going about their daily lives, often in the face of seismic change – that make *Manufactured Landscapes* such a powerful record of a world heading in the wrong direction.

INTO ETERNITY

MICHAEL MADSEN; DENMARK/
FINLAND/SWEDEN/ITALY;
2010; 75 MINS

A fascinating overview of a scientific project that encompasses the environment, philosophy, linguistics and speculative theory, Michael Madsen's film grapples with the legacy of nuclear power and the danger it poses for generations to come. Initially focusing on the construction of a vast network of mineshafts capable of storing nuclear waste, the film eventually turns its attention to finding a way to safeguard a future world from this toxic waste.

In 2004, construction started on the world's first spent nuclear fuel repository, in Finland. Based near the Olkiluoto Nuclear Power Plant, on the country's west coast, Onkalo (which means 'cavity') is a vast network of tunnels, channels and chambers, built into a granite bedrock that has remained stable for 1.8 billion years. Designed as a series of vast zigzagging shafts that work their way down to five kilometres beneath the ground, the main artery branches out into smaller alleys that lead to hundreds of storage spaces. Eventually, each space will store 12 fuel assemblies, placed into a boron steel canister enclosed in a copper capsule and packed with bentonite clay.

Employing an otherworldly tone, the beautifully composed tracking shots that journey into the tunnel echo the combination of solemnity and wonder that propelled Stanley Kubrick's *2001: A Space Odyssey* (1968). But the physical demands of constructing this labyrinthine underworld pale against the challenge of warning future societies of the danger contained within it. What can be done to prevent future species from entering the tunnels? As Kraftwerk's 'Radioactivity' plays on the soundtrack, we are informed that spent nuclear fuel has a lifespan of 100,000 years. The oldest known form of human communication – cave paintings – are only tens of thousands of years old. What sign would constitute danger and could it prevent future archaeologists from opening the tunnel the way we ventured into the pyramids of Egypt? Or would it be safer for grass to grow over the tunnels' entrance and hope that it remained undiscovered? It's a fascinating conundrum with no clear answer, but is aptly summed up by one expert, who wryly concludes: 'When you do a project like this, you must state what you know and you must state that you know what you know that you don't know, and also what you don't know that you don't know.'

ALSO SEE

Lessons of Darkness
(p.141)

Countdown to Zero
(Lucy Walker; 2010)
A chilling analysis of the dangers posed by unchecked nuclear weapons and fissile materials in an age of political instability.

Cave of Forgotten Dreams
(Werner Herzog; 2010)
A 3D journey into France's Chauvet caves, which feature some of the world's oldest primitive paintings.

Homo Sapiens
(Nikolaus Geyrhalter; 2016)
An eerily beautiful and unsettling series of portraits of places long abandoned by their occupants.

I KNEW FROM THE BEGINNING THAT IT WOULD MAKE SENSE TO THINK OF THE

Michael Madsen

DOCUMENTARY AS A SCIENCE FICTION FILM SHOT TODAY.

THE DUST BOWL

KEN BURNS;
US; 2012; 229 MINS

ALSO SEE

Dawson City: Frozen Time
(p.126)

An Inconvenient Truth
(Davis Guggenheim; 2006)
Al Gore's lecture-as-a-film is a striking warning about the environmental threat we pose to the planet.

The Great Flood
(Bill Morrison; 2012)
Footage of the devastating 1927 Mississippi flood explores our relationship with the natural world.

The Roosevelts: An Intimate History
(Ken Burns; 2014)
A portrait of the US president and his wife, who introduced a system of changes to help rural communities in the 1930s.

Over the course of four decades, Ken Burns has chronicled events, eras, cultures and conflicts spanning two centuries of American life. His documentaries are expansive and often exhaustive in length. *The Dust Bowl*, a two-part study of the environmental disaster that hit the prairies of North America during the depression years of the 1930s, is one of his shortest and most incisive. It is also one of the few films by Burns whose conclusions point to a future that is potentially bleaker than the events he depicts.

The film's primary focus is the Oklahoma Panhandle, an area surrounded by Texas, New Mexico, Colorado and Kansas. It charts how, in the late 1920s, vast parcels of the American prairie were transformed into arable land. The cultivation of wheat was so dramatic, encompassing millions of acres and using methods that made the ground unstable, that disaster loomed. It arrived in winter 1932. The rains that had been constant throughout most of the 1920s stopped falling. Winds picked up and the earth, no longer tethered to the ground by prairie grass, formed vast dust clouds. The worst hit on 14 April 1935, which was memorialized by Woody Guthrie in his song 'The Great Dust Storm' and reported on by Associated Press journalist Robert Geiger, who first made use of the phrase 'dust bowl'.

The film profits from an extraordinary photographic record of the era by some of the greatest photographers of the time, including Dorothea Lange, Arthur Rothstein and Walker Evans. Their images are accompanied by first-hand testimonies of people who endured the storms – with many losing family members to them – and the detritus left in their wake. Throughout, Burns employs his signature filmmaking style, zooming and panning over photographs to draw out specific details or emphasize scale, accompanied by a rousing score.

A chilling record of a man-made environmental disaster and the resilience of a people who lived through it, *The Dust Bowl* ends with discussion of the Ogallala Aquifer, a vast lake beneath the Great Plains that has been tapped for drinking water and agricultural irrigation since the late 1940s. Once depleted, it will take approximately 6,000 years to refill. Charles Shaw, of Cimarron County, Oklahoma, offers a bleak prognosis on the area's future for farmers, and by extension humanity's future on Earth. 'If you lose the water,' he notes, 'you're going to lose the land. And that's it in a nutshell.'

LEVIATHAN

LUCIEN CASTAING-TAYLOR,
VERENA PARAVEL;
UK/US/FRANCE; 2012; 87 MINS

ALSO SEE

Araya
(p.18)

Drifters
(John Grierson; 1929)
An experimental documentary focusing
on the herring fishing industry in Britain.

Sweetgrass
(Ilisa Barbash, Lucien
Castaing-Taylor; 2009)
SEL documents shepherds and
their vast flock of sheep journeying
through Montana.

Aquarela
(Viktor Kossakovsky; 2018)
A dazzling exploration of the way
water moves and interacts with
environments around the world.

Leviathan is an innovative sensorial experience. It records filmmakers' Lucien Castaing-Taylor and Verena Paravel's journey aboard a groundfish trawler in the Atlantic, some 200 miles off the north-eastern seaboard of the US. But in the place of a linear account of daily life, the filmmakers construct an immersive film, free of any conventional narrative structure, that captures the workings of the vessel as it navigates turbulent waters and demands the most of those who work aboard it. At times disorientating, successfully conveying the queasiness experienced while navigating rough seas, *Leviathan* pushes the envelope of filmmaking practice into unchartered creative waters.

The film originated in the Sensory Ethnography Laboratory (SEL), which is run by Castaing-Taylor out of Harvard University. The combined project of the university's departments of Anthropology, and Visual and Environmental Studies, SEL was set up to combine ethnographic studies with an exploration of aesthetics through analogue and digital media practice, as well as installation and performance art. *Leviathan* is the first collaboration between Castaing-Taylor and Paravel, who had previously worked on separate projects at the lab.

The filmmakers initially intended to make a documentary about the land-based workings of the fishing industry, but instead changed their focus to one ship. They made six trips aboard a trawler based out of New Bedford, Massachusetts. (The largest fishing port in the US, New Bedford was once the home of whaling and is where Herman Melville's *Moby Dick* began.) After the loss of their main camera during the first trip, the filmmakers deployed small Go-Pro cameras across the entirety of the boat, from cabins and on deck to the various masts, cranes and nets. They capture teeming life beneath the waves and attempts by seabirds to steal from the catch. The filmmakers' inability to manually finesse the focus of each camera resulted in striking, occasionally haunting, images that were then edited into a compelling montage. Employing a title with roots in the Biblical, mythological and – through Thomas Hobbes' eponymous 1651 treatise – philosophical, the filmmakers eschew specificity in favour of the universal. Their film can be viewed as a rumination on humanity's relationship with the elements, both around the world and through time.

COW

ANDREA ARNOLD;
UK; 2021; 94 MINS

Acclaimed British filmmaker Andrea Arnold's first documentary feature focuses, as its title makes clear, on a cow, named Luma. It charts a year in the animal's life, from her giving birth to a calf, through the daily routine of a dairy farm, to her death. Remaining in close proximity to Luma throughout, save for brief cutaways to other activities on the farm, *Cow* might initially seem an outlier in Arnold's body of work. But the film's intimacy, the way its camera probes rather than observes, finds it of a piece with the writer-director's *Fish Tank* (2009), *American Honey* (2016) and earthy *Wuthering Heights* (2011).

The film opens with Luma delivering her sixth calf. No sooner is the animal born than it is business as usual. There are the various rounds of milking throughout the day, post-natal veterinary check-ups, grazing in surrounding fields and hour after hour spent in one of the barns. A bull mates with her and she gives birth again, athough this time Arnold only shoots Luma's face. Farm hands check on the health of the new-born while the mother is returned to her routine. Then, one morning, Luma is led to a separate barn and killed with a gunshot to the head.

Arnold's film is no rosy portrait of a pastoral idyll. But neither is it a soulless or grim affair. There is much humour, some of it aimed at nature documentaries that strive to anthropomorphize their subject. Cinematographer Magda Kowalczyk, whose camera is positioned so close to Luma that the animal gives it an occasional bump with her head, lingers on her eyes. Are we meant to read something in them? An occasional shot of a plane flying overhead finds editor Rebecca Lloyd slyly cutting back to Luma, fancifully implying that she is considering escape to pastures new. And the footage of Luma being mounted by a bull cuts to a firework display, reminiscent of the oh-so-coy sex scene between Cary Grant and Grace Kelly in Alfred Hitchcock's *To Catch a Thief* (1955). The playfulness recedes as Luma grows weary with age and exertion. Arnold's compassion remains, albeit free of sentimentality. It is accompanied by a sense of unease, not just regarding the treatment of animals, but the exploitation of sexuality that has been a key element in much of the filmmaker's work.

179

CRIME

&

INJUSTICE

THE THIN BLUE LINE

ERROL MORRIS;
US; 1988; 101 MINS

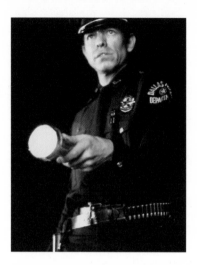

Errol Morris' influential documentary investigates the murder of Texas police officer Robert Wood on 29 November 1976, which led to the wrongful conviction of Randall Dale Adams. A key element in Adams' eventual release, *The Thin Blue Line* is acclaimed for its use of dramatic re-enactment and incorporation of Philip Glass' propulsive score, and stands in contrast to the conventions of Direct Cinema.

Adams' conviction rested on the testimony of juvenile offender David Harris, statements from three questionable witnesses and the myopic investigation of a group of Dallas police detectives. It is made clear that interest in charging Adams over Harris stemmed from state law preventing adolescents receiving the death penalty. After being found guilty, Adams was assessed by court-appointed psychiatrists John Holbrook and James Grigson, who confirmed that he would likely kill again if he was ever released and therefore should be executed.

Morris initially intended to make a documentary about Grigson, known as Doctor Death for his success rate in securing executions. The psychiatrist suggested Morris research the trials he had participated in, which is how he encountered Adams. Like his early films *Gates of Heaven* (1978) and *Vernon, Florida* (1981), *The Thin Blue Line* highlights Morris' interest in the idiosyncrasies of human behaviour, which are borne out through his intercutting of interviews he conducted with Adams, Harris, the investigating officers, defence and prosecution attorneys, and various other witnesses. (Morris would subsequently develop his interviewing technique with the introduction of the 'Interrotron', a variation of the teleprompter that allowed subjects to address the camera directly, but instead of a lens they would see the filmmaker's face.)

The interviews, skilfully intercut with supplementary material from TV reports, newspapers and radio, and archive footage are structured around Morris' repeated and multi-perspective re-enactment of the crime. His emphasis on this, giving the film the feel of a fictional thriller, was radical for a documentary. It attracted the ire of some critics and more purist documentary filmmakers, who saw it as a betrayal of the form. However, the style proved influential and over subsequent decades would become commonplace. The film also prompted the reopening of Adams' case and its eventual dismissal in 1989. It cemented the reputation of Morris, who would subsequently become one of US cinema's most distinctive and celebrated filmmakers.

WE CREATE CONCEPTIONS OF REALITY, PICTURES OF REALITY,

Errol Morris

RE-ENACTMENTS – IF YOU LIKE – OF REALITY.

CLOSE-UP

NEMA-YE NAZDIK
ABBAS KIAROSTAMI; IRAN;
1990; 98 MINS

In Iranian filmmaker Abbas Kiarostami's international breakthrough, a prosperous Tehran family are duped by a young man posing as a famous filmmaker. Examining the nature of justice and of the role cinema plays in our lives, Kiarostami cast the participants in this real-life case as themselves. In doing so, he raises questions about truth, reality and the documentary form.

When Mrs Mahrokh Ahankhah sat next to Hossein Sabzian on a bus and commented on his reading the screenplay to Mohsen Makhmalbaf's *The Cyclist* (1989), Sabzian claimed to be the filmmaker. He was subsequently invited to the Ahankhah household, promised to feature them in his next film – even going so far as to stage rehearsals with them – and borrowed a small amount of money from Mehrdad, one of the sons. But his ruse was soon uncovered. The police were called. Sabzian was arrested and a magazine article about the case was published prior to his trial.

On reading about the case, Kiarostami met with Sabzian and the Ahankhahs, convincing them to appear in his film. He persuaded the cleric judge to allow him to film the trial, even moving the date of it to accommodate his filming schedule. He also asked Sabzian questions during the proceedings. Many of the speeches Sabzian gave in court, albeit based on previous conversations, were written by Kiarostami. The filmmaker then recreated the incident on the bus and events leading to the arrest. The film's denouement, a meeting between Sabzian, the real Mohsen Makhmalbaf and Mr Ahankhah, was all pre-organized by the filmmaker, although the emotions expressed are real. Kiarostami even shot one scene with the sound intentionally missing, to add to the 'realness' of the enterprise.

Close-Up exists between documentary and drama. It's a creatively rich hinterland that allows Kiarostami to explore the desire of a poor, single father, living with his mother and one of his children, to have his existence acknowledged by others in the world, even if it requires him to lie. In turn, Sabzian's story allowed Kiarostami to explore the relationship between cinema and everyday life. It's an approach that would influence countless other filmmakers around the world and helped cement Kiarostami as one of contemporary cinema's leading figures.

THE GREATEST DOCUMENTARY ON FILMMAKING I HAVE EVER SEEN.

OFFICER'S STATION

YOU DO THINGS, ULTIMATELY, BECAUSE YOU BELIEVE IN THEM, BECAUSE YOU'RE ARMED WITH A SET OF QUESTIONS.

AILEEN WUORNOS: THE SELLING OF A SERIAL KILLER

NICK BROOMFIELD;
UK; 1992; 87 MINS

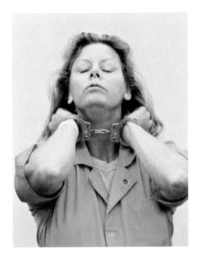

ALSO SEE

Capturing the Friedmans
(p.190)

The Chair
(Robert Drew; 1963)
Drew's film captures the intensity of
attempts by the attorneys of convicted
African American prisoner Paul Crump
to overturn his death sentence.

Waiting for Fidel
(Michael Rubbo; 1974)
A major inspiration for Broomfield, a film
crew record their attempts to interview
Cuban leader Fidel Castro.

Girlhood
(Liz Garbus; 2003)
A raw and unflinching portrait of life
in prison for two female inmates at a
Maryland juvenile detention centre.

Nick Broomfield's first film about Aileen Wuornos is an impassioned critique of the US justice system and those who seek to profit from it. Combining a sobering portrait of a prisoner on death row with often unintended humorous asides that have become a hallmark of his work, Broomfield's film challenges the media image of Aileen Wuornos, and in doing so berates a system that is shown to be venal in its exercise of power.

Between 1989 and 1990, Wuornos shot and killed seven men at point blank range. A sex worker, she claimed that all the men had either sexually assaulted her or attempted to do so, and that her actions were taken in self-defence. She was found guilty on six counts of murder and sentenced to death in 1992; it was carried out on 9 October 2002.

Broomfield's film grew out of his interest in interviewing what US media outlets were describing as the country's first female serial killer. But his intended profile of Wuornos soon focused on the people 'protecting' her; in particular, Steve Glazer, Wuornos' inexperienced and inept attorney, and Arlene Pralle, a born-again Christian who championed Wuornos after hearing about her case on TV. Together, they demanded $25,000 from Broomfield to interview her. (The filmmaker is eventually seen paying $10,000 to Glazer.) There was also the circus of lawyers, police officers and agents who were selling film and TV rights to their role in Wuornos' case.

If Broomfield's earlier work was inspired by cinéma vérité, his films from *Chicken Ranch* (1982) on saw him play an increasingly visible on-screen presence, often as a counterpoint or provocation to his subjects. It was a style that subsequently influenced filmmakers such as Michael Moore and Louis Theroux. If some of his films exude a playful side, Broomfield's account of Wuornos' case becomes darker and more sobering as it progresses. When he was subpoenaed to appear in Wuornos' defence in an appeal against her death sentence, Broomfield and co-director Joan Churchill recorded what took place. *Aileen: Life and Death of a Serial Killer* (2003) features his last encounter with Wuornos, just prior to her execution. It highlights the severity of her psychological state and channels its ire towards the US legal system, which Broomfield sums up as 'completely barbaric'.

4 LITTLE GIRLS

SPIKE LEE;
US; 1997; 102 MINS

ALSO SEE

13th
(p.81)

Integration Report 1
(Madeleine Anderson; 1960)
An account of racism across America
and the rise of Civil Rights activity by one
of the first Black female US filmmakers.

When the Levees Broke:
A Requiem in Four Acts
(Spike Lee; 2006)
A comprehensive account of the
aftermath of hurricane Katrina's impact
on New Orleans and the aftermath.

MLK/FBI
(Sam Pollard; 2020)
A focus on the FBI's surveillance of
Martin Luther King, Jr and their efforts
to infiltrate the Civil Rights Movement.

Spike Lee's moving feature documentary debut tells the story of a racist attack on a church in Birmingham, Alabama, that resulted in the deaths of four young African American girls and sparked national outrage. Combining the testimony of family members alongside a history of the events that led to the rise of the Civil Rights Movement, *4 Little Girls* is less combative than many of Lee's narrative features, but its accumulation of detail nevertheless results in a searing portrait of racial injustice.

On Sunday 15 September 1963, a bomb was planted beneath the steps on the east side of the 16th Street Baptist Church in Birmingham, a venue known as a rallying point for civil rights activities. Addie Mae Collins (14), Cynthia Wesley (14), Carole Robertson (14) and Carol Denise McNair (11) were in the basement when the device exploded. Opening with Joan Baez's rendition of 'Birmingham Sunday', *4 Little Girls* initially details each girl's family life at the time, framing them as innocents who were only just beginning to realize the challenges they faced as Black children in the Deep South. Lee then broadens the film's scope, beyond Birmingham, to detail the rise of the Civil Rights Movement and the corresponding increase of violence aimed at Black communities throughout the Deep South and across the US.

The girl's killers are mentioned late in the film, but Lee spends little time on them, athough he does link them to powerful figures such as 'Bull' Connor, Birmingham's racist Commissioner of Public Safety and Governor George Wallace. When one of the killers' defence attorneys attempts to suggest life in Birmingham was peaceful during this era, he juxtaposes their comments with footage of Ku Klux Klan members and their children dressed in white Klan outfits, and a photograph of a lynched Black man with a sign around his neck that reads 'This nigger voted'.

4 Little Girls brought back into focus a crime that shocked a nation, highlighting its role in speeding up passage of the 1964 Civil Rights Act. But Lee never loses focus on Addie, Cynthia, Carole and Carol, daughters and sisters, who were robbed of a full life.

BUS 174

ÔNIBUS 174
JOSÉ PADILHA, FELIPE LACERDA;
BRAZIL; 2002; 133 MINS

In the middle of the afternoon on 12 June 2000, 21-year-old Sandro Barbosa do Nascimento boarded a bus in central Rio de Janeiro. Armed with a pistol, he took its passengers hostage. The siege lasted four hours and was watched live on television by millions. José Padilha and Felipe Lacerda's film reconstructs the event from those broadcasts, contextualizing it within the city's recent past, the actions of a notorious law enforcement agency and the story of a young man whose crime was the final chapter in a short and grim life. The film also examines the role that television news plays in our lives and how it has become indivisible from mass entertainment.

Nascimento was being pursued by a police officer when he boarded the bus. It wasn't long before more police arrived on the scene, along with a multitude of TV cameras – the bus had stopped directly outside the headquarters of TV Globo, the country's main terrestrial channel. A cordon failed to hold back the cameras and so a domestic audience of an estimated 35 million were glued to their TVs as the situation – with cameras extraordinarily close to the action – edged towards its tragic conclusion: one hostage was fatally shot and Nascimento was killed by officers as they transported him to a police station.

From its breathtaking opening aerial shot over Rio, highlighting both the economic disparity and physical proximity between rich and poor in the city, *Bus 174* examines what took place through the prism of a society riven by violence towards ethnic groups, and its dispossessed and homeless. Many watching the siege would have understood the meaning of Nascimento's cries to the police, 'Didn't you kill my friends at Candelária?' He was referring to the 1993 massacre of homeless children outside the city's Candelária Church by an armed group that included police officers. Nascimento was there and survived. Those who knew him say he never recovered from it.

Bus 174 conveys the tension of a live broadcast, but also highlights the role the media played in re-enforcing xenophobic stereotypes of the country's ethnic minorities. It also questions the very notion of what stands for entertainment, on the cusp of an age when reality television would become all-pervasive.

ALSO SEE

Man on Wire
(p.113)

Streetwise
(Martin Bell; 1984)
A startling account of the lives of nine teenagers on the streets of Seattle.

One Day in September
(Kevin Macdonald; 1999)
An overview of the events surrounding the hostage-taking of Israeli athletes at the 1972 Munich Olympics.

Children Underground
(Edet Belzberg; 2001)
Life on the streets for five of the thousands of homeless children living in the Romanian capital of Bucharest.

CAPTURING THE FRIEDMANS

ANDREW JARECKI;
US; 2003; 107 MINS

The title of Andrew Jarecki's riveting attempt to redraw the parameters of the crime documentary plays out on a number of levels. There is the criminal case levelled against Arnold Friedman and his youngest son Jesse. Following the men's arrest, eldest son David bought a video camera and recorded his family's freefall into a state of rage and bitter recrimination. Finally, Jarecki attempts to piece together what took place and in doing so frames the Friedmans' case within the context of a society caught in the grip of hysteria over widespread child abuse.

In 1987, the US Postal Service intercepted a package containing child pornography. A subsequent investigation into its recipient, respected high school computer teacher Arnold Friedman, escalated when dozens of students claimed they had been abused by him and Jesse. Both were eventually convinced by their attorneys to plead guilty. Jarecki first heard about the case from David, who was one of the subjects of the filmmaker's documentary short about child entertainers in New York. *Capturing the Friedmans* combines David's footage with contemporary interviews filmed by Jarecki, with surviving family members, law enforcement officers involved in the case and a number of Friedman's former students.

There is no doubt over the original charge levelled at Arnold. He freely admitted to paedophilic desires. But as Jarecki's film delves deeper into the Long Island police department's investigation, discrepancies appear. One officer's claim that some rooms contained stacks of pornographic magazines is not reflected in photographs taken at the time. And the handling of the victims led some, including an experienced journalist who had been investigating child abuse claims on a national level, to question the probity of the unit's procedures in dealing with minors, which included the dubious use of hypnosis. There was even evidence of some parents coercing others to get their children to claim they had been abused in order to strengthen their case against Jesse and Arnold. All the while, father and son remained steadfast in maintaining that they did nothing to the children.

David's footage of his family's meltdown is agonizing to watch, and their willingness to play up to the camera is bizarre at times – a stark contrast to their restraint in subsequent interviews. Taken together, these strands underpin the film's central theme, of the unreliability of memory and the slippery nature of truth.

ALSO SEE

Stories We Tell
(p.48)

Crumb
(Terry Zwigoff; 1994)
A wry and affecting portrait of the cartoonist Robert Crumb and his eccentric family.

Waco: The Rules of Engagement
(William Gazecki; 1997)
An investigative account of the failed operation to raid the heavily fortified Branch Davidian compound in Texas.

Weiner
(Josh Kriegman, Elyse Steinberg; 2016)
An as-it-happens record of Anthony Weiner's scandal-ridden attempts to run for mayor of New York City in 2013.

IT'S TIME FOR THE STORY TO BE TOLD
AND DON'T FORGET, [THE FAMILY] LIKE PERFORMING,

Andrew Jarecki

THEY LIKE THE LIMELIGHT.

SERIAL

Serial crime documentaries have long been a staple of non-fiction television programming. The rapid growth of podcasting and streaming services has only seen them proliferate. And without the limitations of network television or programming schedules, streamers have been quick to commission true-crime stories that benefit from lengthier running times.

Crime pays very handsomely when it comes to non-fiction 'entertainment'. But finding the formula that attracts audiences is key. *Serial* (2014), the 12-episode podcast produced by the popular weekly radio show 'This American Life' became a landmark in this genre. With a lengthy overall running time and a structure that allowed those working on it to delve into a crime in forensic detail, it is the standard by which all other real-life audio documentaries are judged. It was natural that streamers, with their unlimited capacity, would embrace a similar format.

The Staircase (2004–18) was an early example of the potential for deep-dive investigations into a single crime. Detailing the case of Michael

Above: *The Staircase* (2004–18)
Opposite: Robert Durst, subject of *The Jinx* (2015)

Peterson, who was accused of murdering his wife, it transformed from a one-off film into a 13-part series. Each episode emerged in tandem with new revelations in the case over the course of 14 years. But it was *Making a Murderer* (2015–18, p.198) that defined the template of the modern serial crime documentary. Like *The Staircase*, the story of Steven Avery proved compelling enough to span an extensive series, with an eventual running time of almost 20 hours. Around the same time, *Capturing the Friedmans* (2003, p.190) director Andrew Jarecki explored the case of Robert Durst, in *The Jinx* (2015). Together, these series have proven influential over subsequent crime documentaries.

A lengthier running time also allows a film to broaden its scope. Ezra Edelman's *O.J.: Made in America* (2016, p.200) is a perfect example of an in-depth exploration of one case as a way of highlighting wider themes prevalent in society. It's a tactic that was subsequently employed by *Stephen: The Murder that Changed a Nation* (2018, p.204) and Steve McQueen and James Rogan's *Uprising* (2021).

CRIMES

SISTERS IN LAW

KIM LONGINOTTO,
FLORENCE AYISI; CAMEROON/UK;
2005; 104 MINS

ALSO SEE

Stephen:
The Murder that Changed a Nation
(p.204)

Rafea: Solar Mama
(Mona Eldaief, Jehane Noujaim; 2012)
A Jordanian Bedouin travels to the
Barefoot College solar programme
in India, to learn how to harness
the sun's power.

Salma
(Kim Longinotto; 2013)
A profile of the Indian Tamil poet, activist
and politician, who campaigns for
women's and transgender rights.

Sabaya
(Hogir Hirori; 2021)
An account of a group who risk their
lives to save women being held
by ISIS in Syria.

Sisters in Law focuses on the work of state prosecutor Vera Ngassa and court president Beatrice Ntuba as they enforce law in Kumba Town, Cameroon. Women and girls appear to be the victims in many of the cases that pass across their desks, and each case is seen as an opportunity to change a patriarchal mindset, acknowledging the rights of all before the law. Kim Longinotto and co-director Florence Ayisi's intimate portrait exudes warmth towards its subjects, while the two officials' intelligence, wit, compassion and unwavering belief in the importance of what they do makes their daily life compelling viewing.

The film focuses on four cases: a woman fighting for custody of her child; the sexual assault of a nine-year-old girl; a family member arrested for beating her infant niece; and a woman seeking a way out of an abusive marriage. Each case is tried under Sharia law. It's not so much in these officials' adherence to it that the film details, but how Ngassa and Ntuba work with it to address the breadth of inequality women experience in society. The male defendants are soon made aware that their gender offers them no leniency or privilege in the court. Longinotto and Ayisi show less concern with the men, focusing more on how Ngassa and Ntuba use their position to support women, leading by example and showing that empowerment is possible. Nowhere is this more evident than in one of the film's final scenes, when Ntuba introduces her class of law students to two Muslim women who saw their husbands successfully convicted of spousal abuse, the first successful convictions for the crime in 17 years. Likewise, in the case of Manka, the infant brutally abused by her aunt, the film shows Ntuba's firmness in exercising the law but also a desire to rehabilitate in order to prevent similar incidents happening in the future. She expresses the utmost concern for Manka, ensuring she finds a stable and safe home environment to recover from the abuse she has endured.

Like her earlier *Divorce Iranian Style* (1998), *The Day I Will Never Forget* (2002) and subsequent *Rough Aunties* (2008) and *Pink Saris* (2010), *Sisters in Law* finds Longinotto steering a course between documenting the strictures of societal codes and laws, and the individuals and groups intent on making women's lives better within them. It is another vital film in Longinotto's essential body of work.

REBELS ARE OFTEN WOMEN.

Kim Longinotto

195

MEA MAXIMA CULPA: SILENCE IN THE HOUSE OF GOD

ALEX GIBNEY;
US/UK; 2012; 106 MINS

An investigation into abuse by a priest at a Milwaukee school for deaf children broadens out to highlight a rot that has spread throughout the Catholic church. Alex Gibney's searing indictment of criminal negligence encompasses every corner of the world's largest organization, including the Vatican.

Gibney's film initially focuses on four men, Terry Kohut, Gary Smith, Pat Kuehn and Arthur Budzinski, who attended St John's School for the Deaf between 1953 and 1970. Each was subject to sexual abuse by Father Lawrence Murphy, who first arrived at the school in the 1950s. As early as 1963, an attempt was made to alert a visiting priest, who raised the issue with his superiors but was silenced, leaving these boys, along with many others over subsequent years, to suffer.

Mea Maxima Culpa employs brief dramatic sequences early on to emphasize the oppressive world the boys endured. But like Gibney's Oscar-winning War on Terror exposé *Taxi to the Dark Side* (2007), the film soon shifts from its forensic account of what took place at the school to encompass the wider landscape of a global organization that abused its privileged position to cover the multitude of crimes committed by figures of authority. It draws on earlier investigations, along with testimonies by former priests, monks and officials, to show how the Vatican has paid off, coerced and bullied people into remaining silent, as well as reassigning priests to other parishes where they continued abusing. In 1947, it even set up an organization, the Congregation of the Servants of the Paraclete, which at one point considered purchasing a Caribbean island to relocate offenders. The long list of abusers included one of Pope John Paul II's most trusted advisers – and, significantly, a major Vatican fundraiser – while the subsequent Pontiff, Pope Benedict, was for years the head of the Congregation of the Doctrine of the Faith, which amassed all the information regarding priests' offences, yet did nothing. Gibney corrals all these details into a clear narrative, while never losing focus on the four men from St John's, whose battle to make their voices heard was a vital part of a sea change in attitudes towards the Catholic Church.

ALSO SEE

Five Broken Cameras
(p.148)

Deliver Us From Evil
(Amy Berg; 2006)
An account of the crimes of Irish Catholic priest Oliver O'Grady, guilty of abusing children for 20 years.

The Keepers
(Ryan White; 2017)
An investigation into the disappearance of a nun at a Catholic girl's school in 1969.

Procession
(Robert Greene; 2021)
Six survivors of childhood abuse at the hands of Catholic priests undergo dramatherapy treatment.

... PEOPLE IN INSTITUTIONS ... NEED TO BE HELD ACCOUNTABLE FOR A CRIME THAT THEY COMMIT,

Alex Gibnev

PERIOD.

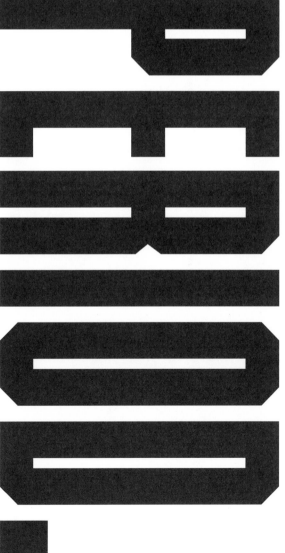

MAKING A MURDERER

LAURA RICCIARDI, MOIRA DEMOS;
US; 2015-18; 1,251 MINS

In 1985, Steven Avery was convicted of rape and sentenced to 32 years in prison, even though 16 eyewitness accounts placed him 40 miles away from the crime scene. Advances in DNA testing eventually saw his conviction overturned. However, shortly after he began civil proceedings for his wrongful conviction, he was arrested on a murder charge. Laura Ricciardi and Moira Demos' investigation, shot over the course of 10 years, unravels these events and in doing so set the benchmark for future serial documentaries.

Painstakingly researched, *Making a Murderer* is a testament to the values of the traditional narration-free documentary. The series relies solely on the testimony of those involved in the case and the use of extensive archive footage, drawn from TV interviews and reports, courtroom video and depositions, and an array of other sources that not only lay out the details of the cases, but construct a fascinating portrait of small-town life.

Opening with Avery's acquittal and release from prison in 2003, Ricciardi and Demos trawl through the prosecution's case, uncovering actions by the police and local prosecutors implying gross misconduct. From there, the series delves into the second charge and Avery's failed attempts to clear his name, with prosecutors appearing hell-bent on proving his guilt. (It is made clear that the second charge is regarded by some as a vengeful tactic prompted by Avery's lawsuit.) This includes the lengthy interrogation of Avery's 16-year-old cousin, who possesses limited mental faculties, with no parent, legal guardian or attorney present. It's on his testimony that the prosecution rest much of their case and where the filmmakers question the use of coercion to obtain a confession.

In addition to their forensic examination of the case, the filmmakers turn their attention to the media's sensationalist coverage. Just as Nick Broomfield was scathing of the way in which Aileen Wuornos' trial and execution was presented as an entertainment (p.186) two decades before, Ricciardi and Demos highlight the damage done to Avery's case by news channels whose only interest lies in an attention-catching headline and a ratings-friendly story. *Making a Murderer* is as much a critique of the perniciousness of the media as it is a reminder of the fallibility of the law and the individuals that enforce it.

ALSO SEE

The Thin Blue Line
(p.182)

The Staircase
(Jean-Xavier de Lestrade; 2004–18)
A detailed account of the case against Michael Peterson, charged with murdering his wife, Kathleen.

Dear Zachary: A Letter to a Son About His Father
(Kurt Kuenne; 2008)
Kuenne produced this portrait of Andrew Bagby, killed by the woman who gave birth to their child, so that his son would have a record of him.

West of Memphis
(Amy Berg; 2012)
Berg details the failure of the justice system in the wrongful conviction of three youths for murder.

O.J.: MADE IN AMERICA

EZRA EDELMAN;
US; 2016; 467 MINS

ALSO SEE

I Am Not Your Negro
(p.84)

Eyes on the Prize
(Henry Hampton; 1987–90)
A serial documentary on the American
Civil Rights Movement from
1954 to 1965.

Jackie Robinson
(Ken Burns, Sarah Burns,
David McMahon; 2016)
An overview of the baseball legend's
career and the racism he faced
and stood up to.

LA 92
(Daniel Lindsay, T.J. Martin; 2017)
A record of the six-day riot that took
place in Los Angeles County following
the acquittal of the LAPD officers who
were filmed beating Rodney King.

There are few better examples of the blurred line between the theatrical documentary feature and serial documentary than Ezra Edelman's impressive examination of O.J. Simpson's life and crimes. Made as a five-part series for television by ESPN, the eight-hour film was also released into cinemas. It received two Primetime Emmy Awards and the Academy Award for Best Documentary. But the scope of Edelman's film travels beyond the rollercoaster ride of Simpson's sporting and entertainment career, the murders of Nicole Brown Simpson and Ron Goldman, and the ex-football star's subsequent conviction for a robbery in Las Vegas. As its title suggests, the film regards Simpson as a product of a culture in which the allure of celebrity and greed moulded O.J., his success story transforming into a dark and twisted take on the American Dream.

Edelman's film presents a detailed linear account of Simpson's life, locating it within the wider context of the country's troubled history of racism. It moves from the 1965 Watts Riots and the record of an infamously prejudiced LAPD to the riots that followed the jury verdict in the trial of three police officers charged with beating Rodney King; that result likely influenced the outcome of Simpson's own trial for the murders of Nicole and Goldman. Edelman amassed a vast trove of archive footage and interviews with people who knew Simpson throughout his life, as well as those involved on both sides of the murder and subsequent robbery trials. A key factor in the 467-minute film's success is how Edelman sets the pace – detailing key moments in the life of Simpson and the history of Los Angeles, while never losing control of the narrative's forward momentum.

Simpson comes across as a charismatic figure, an exceptional athlete, a mediocre actor and a man whose pursuit of success and fame, and attempts throughout his life to fit into a mostly white strata of society, brought out a bitterness that turned to rage. It eventually manifested itself as jealousy towards Nicole, both during the latter stages of their marriage and after they had separated. Alongside this, Edelman continues to chart the simmering tensions amongst the LAPD and ethnic communities throughout Los Angeles.

O.J.: Made in America leaves its audience to decide on Simpson's guilt. But the film suggests that when a city is so riven with prejudice, was anyone involved in the case, or those watching as every facet of it unfolded – from the live coverage of Simpson's pursuit along a Los Angeles freeway to the lengthy trial – really expecting justice to be served?

WE TALK ABOUT O.J. AS THOUGH THE STORY IS O.J.

THE STORY IS

O.J. & US.

Journalist Celia Farber

LOUIS THEROUX: DARK STATES

DAN CHILD, JAMIE PICKUP,
JASON MASSOT;
UK; 2017; 176 MINS

Since the late 1990s, Louis Theroux has written and presented one-off and serial documentaries encompassing politics, crime, celebrity and social issues. With his avuncular, occasionally bemused temperament, he established himself as a persuasive interviewer. The three-part *Dark States* found him exploring the underbelly of US life – a society awash with sex, guns and substance abuse. Arguably his bleakest series, it is also one of his most compassionate.

'Heroin Town' journeys to the heart of an out-of-control drug epidemic in Huntington, West Virginia, where death from overdose is a daily sight for the city's paramedics, and the chronic impact of powerful prescription painkillers has upended conventional statistics regarding the 'typical' user. 'Sex Trafficking in Houston' finds Theroux prowling the streets of Texas' most populous city with vice cops and prostitutes. Key to the programme is his attempt to unravel the complex relationship between prostitutes and their pimps, which some of his interviewees admit is often abusive yet relies on a level of intimacy that they come to regard as a form of family. And in 'Murder in Milwaukee', Theroux visits a city plagued by gun-related homicides, highlighting the profound distrust between the African American community and law enforcement agencies. (As the brother of a young man shot and killed by an officer in disputed circumstances notes: 'It's not white on Black, it's blue on Black.')

Combining voiceover commentary and on-screen interviews, the effectiveness of *Dark States*, like many of his programmes, lies in the apparent ease by which Theroux encourages people to talk on camera. From two prostitutes who confide in him, to the cops and the families of gun victims in Milwaukee, the interviewees' frankness is what makes this series so compelling. It is at its most powerful in 'Heroin Town'. Theroux's encounters with addicts are sympathetic and, on occasion, unbearably honest, as he highlights how addiction to prescription medication, and other addictions stemming from them, has cut like a scythe through modern American life, devastating families and communities. Theroux's reaction to those he encounters betrays an ire with a system that has knowingly permitted – and often played a role in – the wanton destruction of so many lives.

... THE PEOPLE YOU MIGHT THINK OF AS 'OTHER' CAN BE QUITE RELATABLE.

Louis Theroux

BUT I DON'T THINK I GIVE THEM A PLATFORM UNCRITICALLY.

MY SON'S BEEN MURDERED

AND NONE OF THESE OFFICERS, THE JUSTICE SYSTEM, THE POLITICIANS, NOBODY CARED.

Doreen Lawrence

STEPHEN: THE MURDER THAT CHANGED A NATION

JAMES ROGAN;
UK; 2018; 180 MINS

The murder of 18-year-old Stephen Lawrence on 22 April 1993 became a focal point of opposition to a rising tide of racism in the UK. But the subsequent handling of the case by the police revealed prejudices that ran deep through some of the country's institutions. A comprehensive and moving account of Stephen's short life, and of a family determined to seek justice, as well as a detailed analysis of the investigation into the murder, James Rogan's three-part documentary aired on the 25th anniversary of the crime. It presents an unsettling portrait of what life was like for Black communities living in Britain in the early 1990s.

The film opens with Stephen's mother Doreen Lawrence telling her story, of coming to Britain in 1963, marrying Neville and having Stephen. The couple acknowledge the racism that was present in everyday life, but its impact was mostly peripheral – until Stephen was attacked by six white youths while waiting at a bus stop with his friend Duwayne Brooks. Racial slurs were heard as the gang approached. Stephen was pushed to the ground and stabbed twice. He got up and tried to run away but collapsed after a short distance. By the time he reached a hospital, he was dead.

The film weaves its way through the botched investigations, attempts to stymie the Lawrences' campaign for justice, and chilling surveillance footage of suspects espousing their racist beliefs and practising the act of stabbing. The film seamlessly intercuts between archive footage and contemporary interviews. Brooks, in particular, is a tragic, pained figure; his only failing was to be a terrified boy who ran away, momentarily leaving his friend behind. (It's something that Doreen, understandably, cannot completely forgive. More painfully, neither can Duwayne.) As the film progresses, attention shifts to Detective Chief Inspector Clive Driscoll's investigation, his unwavering belief in justice separates him from the blind prejudice of many colleagues.

Co-produced by *Senna* (2010) and *Amy* (2015, p.122) director Asif Kapadia, *Stephen: The Murder that Changed a Nation* eschews voiceover narration, allowing the interviews to drive the narrative. Through it all, the dignity and perseverance of Doreen Lawrence is a constant – a grief-stricken mother who eventually overcame every obstacle in her pursuit of justice.

ALSO SEE

4 Little Girls
(p.188)

Handsworth Songs
(John Akomfrah; 1986)
An account of the 1985 riots in London and Birmingham.

Ultraviolence
(Ken Fero; 2020)
An examination of the deaths of people in police custody in the UK.

Uprising
(Steve McQueen, James Rogan; 2021)
The story of the 1981 New Cross Fire in London and its impact upon the black community.

COLLECTIVE

COLECTIV
ALEXANDER NANAU; ROMANIA;
2019; 109 MINS

A fire in a Romanian nightclub and subsequent newspaper investigation exposed a corrupt political system and led to the collapse of the country's government. Alexander Nanau was already documenting the aftermath of the tragedy when he began filming newspaper *Gazeta Sporturilo*'s investigative team. As it progresses, *Collective* turns its attention to the attempts of an interim government to stem the rot that has taken hold in positions of power. In doing so, the film becomes a chilling portrait of political self-interest, whose relevance reaches far beyond Romania's borders.

On 30 October 2015, a fire broke out at the popular Colectiv nightclub in Bucharest. The club allegedly paid off officials to avoid installing safety measures, such as adequate emergency exits. That night, 27 people died in the fire, with a further 180 injured. Over the course of the next few months, another 37 died in hospital, even though some of the dead had only sustained minor burns. The film opens with a meeting between relatives of the victims, followed by a press conference calling for justice. Nanau then shows footage from inside the club, showing how the fire started and rapidly spread.

Collective initially follows Cătălin Tolontan, a *Gazeta Sporturilo* journalist, who leads the investigation into the hospital deaths. It soon emerges that the disinfectant used to eradicate bacteria had been diluted to the point of being ineffective. It enabled its supplier to increase their profits. And medical officials were receiving kickbacks to ignore it. Shortly after the story breaks, the head of the company producing the disinfectant dies suspiciously in a car crash. The film changes gear when a new health minister is appointed – a seemingly honest man grappling with the escalating scandal and a system that appears rotten to the core.

Nanau's film is a sobering portrait of a society where officials have ridden roughshod over checks and balances, allowing profiteering to decide policymaking, which directly affects the health of the country. It ends with the ousted government returning to power on the back of lies and false promises. More than a record of one country's malfeasance, *Collective* is a chilling reflection of a universal trend that has seen compassion replaced by greed and offers a stark prognosis of where that road leads.

A COP MOVIE

UNA PELÍCULA DE POLICÍAS
ALONSO RUIZPALACIOS; MEXICO;
2021; 107 MINS

Following on from his 2018 heist drama *Museo*, Mexican filmmaker Alonso Ruizpalacios turns his attention to individuals on the other side of the law. Initially resembling a real-life police procedural, *A Cop Movie* gradually develops into something more complex and exhilarating. It blurs the line between documentary and fiction as it chronicles the life of two cops, played for the most part by two actors, then details the challenges inherent in playing a role, before returning to the incident that inspired the film.

Divided into chapters, with each peeling away a layer of artifice, *A Cop Movie* initially focuses on the life and work of professional and romantic partners María Teresa Hernández Cañas and José de Jesús Rodríguez Hernández, known by their colleagues as Teresa and Montoya. We first see them on separate duty – Teresa attending to the delivery of a baby and Montoya patrolling a gay pride march – before they work a shift together in a police car and Teresa faces off against a man who turns out to be a friend of her superior; both soon find their careers in jeopardy because of their unwillingness to bend the law. The film then reveals that the two are actors playing roles. Mónica Del Carmen and Raúl Briones were cast by Ruizpalacios and had to undergo real police training for the film. Each records a video diary of their experiences, which makes up the next section of the film. But then Ruizpalacios reveals that the roles played by the actors are in fact the real-life stories of actual cops Teresa and Montoya, the lines spoken by the actors a verbatim transcript of the two officers' conversations with the filmmaker.

At one point, Montoya/Raúl notes, 'Police officers are like actors... The moment you put on that uniform you take on a huge responsibility. And you have to commit 100%.' The role might be a performance, but the stakes are real and high. Montoya and Teresa have had to cope with a system so rife with corruption – both petty and serious – that safety in their world comes at a price. They have to pay for use of a clean gun or effective body protection. Taking kickbacks and bribes is an accepted form of covering the cost of being a cop. Ruizpalacios' film ponders the notion – and questions the advantages – of being honest in a system where those who aren't are the only ones to profit.

SHORT

FILMS

À PROPOS DE NICE

JEAN VIGO;
FRANCE; 1930;
24 MINS

Jean Vigo's satirical short, made in close collaboration with cinematographer – and Dziga Vertov's brother – Boris Kaufman, is an occasionally surreal portrait of the southern French city, where the director was residing due to ill health. Shot on scraps of film – for some sequences, Kaufman was pushed around Nice in a wheelchair, his camera hidden beneath a blanket – Vigo juxtaposes the leisurely life of the privileged with that of the city's poor and working class. The filmmaker contrasts hotels and tenements, and sunbathers with shots of crocodiles, culminating in the giddy coverage of a carnival. The film's associative editing, accentuating the disparity between haves and have-nots, becomes increasingly pronounced as it progresses. In *À propos de Nice*, Vigo notes, 'A way of life is put on trial. The last gasps of a society so lost in its escapism that it sickens you and makes you sympathetic to a revolutionary solution.'

LAND WITHOUT BREAD

LAS HURDES
LUIS BUÑUEL;
SPAIN; 1933;
30 MINS

After collaborating with Salvador Dalí on the Surrealist classic *Un Chien Andalou* (1929) and following the furore he attracted for his scathingly anti-clerical *l'Age d'Or* (1930), Luis Buñuel turned to the fragmented population of Las Hurdes, a mountainous region to the west of Madrid and near the border with Portugal. The film depicts squalor, death and existence at its starkest. But much of it was staged. A goat falling off a cliff appears to have been shot, while a dead baby may just be asleep. The film outraged the leftist government of the time and would attract similar sentiments from the pro-Franco Falangists later in the decade. But though Buñuel might have exaggerated the plight of the villagers, their quality of life remained far behind that of the rest of the country. As with his previous films, Buñuel's intention here was to outrage, and for that outrage to spark action, which it eventually did.

NIGHT MAIL

HARRY WATT,
BASIL WRIGHT;
UK; 1936;
25 MINS

Night Mail has become one of the defining films of the General Post Office Film Unit, whose output was divided between routine documentaries detailing its work and more experimental fare. Celebrating advances in communication, the film charts the journey of the Postal Special train, which travels between London and Scotland, picking up and dropping off mail along the way. Voiceover narration describes its work, with an army of staff, divided by region across the various carriages, sorting letters and packages. Composer Benjamin Britten's score accompanies the journey and, as the train passes the border into Scotland, poet W.H. Auden's lyrical verses encapsulate the importance of the train to daily life: 'This is the night mail crossing the border / bringing the cheque and the postal order / letters for the rich, letters for the poor / the shop on the corner, or the girl next door.'

LISTEN TO BRITAIN

HUMPHREY
JENNINGS,
STEWART
MCALLISTER; UK;
1942; 20 MINS

Few filmmakers captured life in Britain during the Second World War as effectively as Humphrey Jennings. His audio-visual snapshot of the country, produced by the propaganda unit of the Ministry of Information, was aimed at presenting a united British front to the world some two years into the conflict. It journeys from coastline to countryside and city, music hall to concert hall and school to factory. Beyond the sounds and images, Jennings and co-director Stewart McAllister's film focuses on the faces of the British populace, all engaged in a variety of activities, at work or relaxing, playing in the schoolyard or enjoying an evening at a dancehall. A shot of Nelson's Column cuts to a sailor, the Queen is intercut with a woman at the National Gallery. It's a compelling portrait of a country standing together, in solidarity, against any aggressor.

BLOOD OF THE BEASTS

LE SANG DES
BÊTES
GEORGES FRANJU;
FRANCE; 1949;
22 MINS

Georges Franju's study of slaughterhouses in the French capital opens with children playing and romance in the air. The shots of a young couple embracing appear innocuous. But a surrealist hand is at play. Rather than immerse us immediately in the world of Paris' abattoirs, we're guided through the environs around them. From there, Franju reveals the tools of this trade, detailing them in action as he journeys through three slaughterhouses and – interspersed with more vistas of the city – the killing of a horse (Porte de Vanves), cows and calves (Porte de Pantin) and sheep (La Villette market). The narrator introduces the butchers by name as they industriously carry out their work. One even sings a version of 'La Mer' as they kill, skin and dismember the animals. Franju's juxtaposing this world with the one outside it emphasizes the barbarous cost involved in satisfying a civil society's needs.

DAYBREAK EXPRESS

D.A. PENNEBAKER;
US; 1953;
5 MINS

A phantasmagoria of colour, light and sound, D.A. Pennebaker's joyful evocation of a train journey into Manhattan is set to the titular track by Duke Ellington. Opening on a rising sun, its golden glow enveloping the city skyline, we see a silhouette of a train crossing a bridge and pulling into a station. A frenetic montage of shots signals the start of Ellington's propulsive composition. As it picks up tempo, the train pulls away. Images of the occupants sat in the carriages resemble Saul Leiter's 1950s colour photographs. Buildings whiz by; a thrilling phantom shot has the train speeding through stations; skyscrapers are seen from below; a wide angle lens bends bridges and buildings. Then, as the train nears its destination, the blur of the city is transformed into a kaleidoscope of colours, ending on the red of a stop light. This is the frenetic world of metropolitan life.

THE MAD MASTERS

LES MAÎTRES FOUS
JEAN ROUCH;
FRANCE; 1955;
36 MINS

Jean Rouch's controversial documentary focuses on an annual ceremony performed by the Hauka. A religious sect, popular in West Africa since the 1920s, by the mid-1950s it had approximately 30,000 practising members in the Ghanaian capital of Accra. Rouch was invited to film the event, but first he places it within the context of everyday life in the city, a stark contrast to what transpires at the remote location a few hours away. The ceremony involves participants entering a trance, during which they are believed to be possessed by the spirits of their colonial 'masters', exaggerating their manner as a form of mockery and ridicule. Whatever the intention behind the ceremony – some have questioned Rouch's interpretation, suggesting the ritual was more aligned to gaining approval and status in colonial society – it was deemed unsettling enough to be banned by local authorities and remains one of Rouch's most divisive films.

NIGHT AND FOG

NUIT ET
BROUILLARD
ALAIN RESNAIS;
FRANCE; 1956;
32 MINS

Night and Fog is less a 'document' of the Holocaust than a reflection on what was planned and the horror that resulted from it. It is also a witness to what remains. 'The blood is caked, the cries stilled, the camera now the only visitor,' the narrator's astringent voice informs us. Alternating between footage shot of the camps in the present (colour) and the past (black and white), the film describes their creation and the industrial-scale processing of the people interned in them. It details the designs employed in their construction and the need for a constant flow of inmates to ensure their functioning. Its brevity notwithstanding, Resnais created one of the most important records of what took place. And he ends with a caution to those 'who pretend it all happened only once, at a given time and place. We turn a blind eye to what surrounds us and a deaf ear to humanity's never-ending cry'.

THE HOUSE IS BLACK

KHANEH SIAH AST
FORUGH
FARROKHZAD;
IRAN; 1963;
20 MINS

Forugh Farrokhzad had already published three volumes of poetry when a producer approached her with the offer of making a short film. She chose as her subject a leper colony in northwest Iran, combining footage she shot with a doctor's clinical description of leprosy and its treatment, and her reading from the Old Testament, the Quran and her own poetry, to reflect on the nature and beauty of creation. The film avoids exploitation, but neither is it sentimental. Farrokhzad identifies the pain caused by social stigma – her own experiences as a divorcée attracted criticism in the public eye – and exudes compassion for her subjects. Regarded as one of the first films of the influential Iranian New Wave, with subsequent filmmakers including Abbas Kiarostami, Mohsen Makhmalbaf and Jafar Panahi, Farrokhzad might have become a major force in the country's cinema had she not died in a car accident, aged just 32, in 1967.

LBJ

SANTIAGO
ÁLVAREZ; CUBA;
1968; 18 MINS

Santiago Álvarez employed Hollywood cinema, animation, photojournalism, newspaper clippings, archive footage, popular culture ephemera and any other 'found materials', alongside an eclectic and multi-layered soundtrack, to present a wholesale assault on imperialism, colonialism and racism. Edited together in a style the filmmaker referred to as 'nervous montage', his work reached a trenchant apotheosis with his critique of Lyndon B. Johnson's administration. *LBJ* portrays the 36th US president as a figure gambling with lives, his initials appearing on a slot machine as a link – via the first letter of each name – to the assassinations of Martin Luther King Jr, Bobby Kennedy and John F. Kennedy. The film opens with what appears to be a personal sleight, juxtaposing images from the wedding of Johnson's daughter with photographs from *Playboy* magazine. But *LBJ* is more an attack on the system he is seen to represent. The passage of time has not diminished its provocative power.

POWERS OF TEN

CHARLES AND RAY
EAMES; US;
1977; 9 MINS

Charles and Ray Eames' most popular film, adapted from Kees Boeke's book *Cosmic View*, is little short of wondrous. Accompanied by Elmer Bernstein's electronic score and the dulcet narration of MIT Professor of Physics Philip Morrison, the film journeys to the extremes of two worlds. Opening on a shot one metre wide and one metre above a couple enjoying a lazy picnic on the Chicago shore of Lake Michigan, the film travels 10 times the previous distance every 10 seconds. It reaches 100 million light years before journeying back to its original position, then descending into the man's body until it arrives at quarks in the proton of a carbon atom, at 0.000001 angstroms. The film is of a piece with the Eames' work across a variety of media, which encourages us to look anew at the environment around us, the world at large and the vast expanse of the universe.

TEN MINUTES OLDER

PAR DESMIT
MINUTEM VECAKS
HERZ FRANK;
LATVIA; 1978;
10 MINS

A single continuous shot captures the wonder of cinema, and the innocence and inquisitiveness of childhood. Herz Frank's delightful short records the reactions of a group of children as they watch a 'tale about good and evil'. Their ages vary. One child in the back row looks a little older, two to his right are younger. But Frank's camera is mostly focused on the expressive face of a young boy in the front. It zooms in on him when he first reacts to the show. His emotions change with each passing second, displaying anxiety, fear, distress, curiosity and joy, while the accompanying music adds to the drama. Frank noted that: 'The first rule of a documentary filmmaker is: have the patience to observe life.' *Ten Minutes Older* aligns him with directors like François Truffaut and Abbas Kiarostami, who possessed an extraordinary ability to capture a child's view of the world on film.

GALLIVANT

ANDREW KÖTTING;
UK; 1994; 8 MINS

Andrew Kötting's 1996 feature debut *Gallivant* saw the filmmaker travel the coastline of the UK with his grandmother Gladys and daughter Eden. This earlier short is a trial run of sorts, featuring elements that would not only play out in the feature, but have been present throughout much of the filmmaker's work. There is a fascination with the notion of Englishness or Britishness, which embraces both ancient and contemporary rituals, from evidence of remains that date back to pagan times through to the kitsch attractions of seaside resorts. These signifiers of cultures and attitudes are combined with Kötting's gift for attracting fascinating real-life characters, alongside members of his family. All these disparate elements are then pieced together in a frenetic assembly that resembles a scrapbook of memories and ideas, shot through with the filmmaker's mischievous sense of humour, and reinforcing the notion that identity is a malleable, ever-changing construct.

THE TRAIN STOP

POLUSTANOK
SERGEI LOZNITSA;
UKRAINE; 2000;
25 MINS

Shot in grainy black and white, Sergei Loznitsa's fascinating film opens on a train engine at night. The director then cuts to an exterior shot of a station waiting room, with a stationary figure sat motionless in the doorway. Inside, everyone is asleep. The only sounds are the waiting passengers' breathing and a fly buzzing. It feels timeless, but clothes locate the scene in the present or very recent past and hint at a variety of social backgrounds. Only the centre of the frame is in focus, giving each shot a dreamlike quality. Trains pass through the station, but no one musters. The world carries on without them. That's Loznitsa's point. The film was made in 2000, following the surprise announcement, on the eve of the new millennium, that Boris Yeltsin was stepping down and making way for Vladimir Putin. Was this a moment, Loznitsa asks, that an entire nation slept through?

LIFT

MARC ISAACS; UK;
2001; 25 MINS

Marc Isaacs' generous, compassionate and funny debut captures life in one London residential tower block as residents enter and leave its lift. At first, Isaacs just films people travelling to or from their apartment. But as they get used to him, conversations develop. He occasionally asks questions: 'Did you dream last night?', 'What's on your mind today?', 'What's your best memory of your childhood?' The latter elicits the loveliest responses. A previously drunk Scotsman talks of seeing a golden eagle as a child, while another remembers being the only boy in a recorder recital competition. Cutaways to the lift shaft, where sounds and songs echo, suggest the passing of time. One man keeps bringing food to Isaacs; another claims to have a Jacuzzi in his flat; an elderly woman enjoys the attention of the camera; others discuss their faith. Isaacs only catches fleeting glimpses of these lives, but the moments form a rich and colourful tapestry.

SVYATO

VIKTOR
KOSSAKOVSKY;
RUSSIA; 2005;
45 MINS

The film's title means both 'happy' and 'considered holy'. It's also the shortened version of Svyatoslav, the name of Viktor Kossakovsky's son, who was two when this film was shot. Following Svyato's birth, Kossakovsky covered all the mirrors in his house. Then, with concealed cameras positioned at various points, the filmmaker reveals a large mirror at the end of a corridor. The boy is curious at first, believing he has found a friend. He moves closer to his reflection, engaging with it. Gradually, he becomes aware of the symmetry in their actions and Kossakovsky emerges to confirm his son's suspicions. Continuing the filmmaker's documenting the miracle of the ordinary, *Svyato* was meant to have been the first part of a proposed trilogy under the title *Palindromes*. Instead, Kossakovsky's fascination with mirroring saw him expand his ambitions to encompass the whole globe, with *¡Vivan las Antípodas!* (2011).

THE SOLITARY LIFE OF CRANES

EVA WEBER; UK;
2008; 27 MINS

Eva Weber's film captures the experiences of the London crane operators who enjoy a birds'-eye perspective on the city. They resemble the angels in Wim Wenders' 1987 drama *Wings of Desire*, who eavesdrop on the thoughts, desires and fears of Germany's pre-unified capital. But here, the crane operators can only observe human action and interaction, guessing people's motivations as they go about their daily lives. Weber's film has a poetic quality, both in the way she captures aerial life across the course of the day, but also in the way she intersperses her images with snatches of dialogue by the crane operators. They speak in unison of their feelings, stranded yet liberated by their position in the tiny cabin aloft the towering metal frames. Weber's film is both a paean to a city in constant motion and the quiet life that unfolds above it.

ATLANTICS

ATLANTIQUES
MATI DIOP;
FRANCE; 2009;
16 MINS

A voiceover at the beginning of Mati Diop's powerful short describes a nightmare: 'We were sailing and encountered a phenomenon feared by most... waves as high as tall buildings.' From there, the filmmaker records a group of friends on a beach, discussing how one of them, Serigne, attempted to make his way by boat from Senegal to Spain. The journey was terrifying, he notes, but he would do it again. He does – and dies during the crossing. Diop's film approaches the migrant crisis from the perspective of those who bear its brunt. 'There's nothing but dust in my pockets,' Serigne explains, justifying his decision to journey across treacherous waters on a pirogue as being better than hearing his mother say she has nothing to eat. A friend of Serigne's notes: 'Look at the ocean. It has no borders.' Another responds: 'Yet, it offers no branches to hold on to.'

A GIRL IN THE RIVER: THE PRICE OF FORGIVENESS

SHARMEEN OBAID-CHINOY; US/PAKISTAN; 2015; 40 MINS

Saba, a 19-year-old from the Pakistani city of Gujranwala, was betrothed to Qaiser, with her father's consent. Her uncle decided the marriage was beneath the family and that she should marry his brother-in-law. Instead, Saba and Qaiser secretly wed. Her father and uncle took her away just hours later, swearing on the Quran that no harm would come to her. Instead, they shot her, put her body in a bag and dumped her in a local river. She survived and the two men were arrested. Local elders put pressure on Saba and her new family to forgive her father and uncle, which eventually saw all charges against them dropped. Sharmeen Obaid-Chinoy's film is a quietly damning indictment of a system where, as Saba's pro bono lawyer notes, 'women are at a great social and institutional disadvantage'. There is no great victory here, just a plea for change and the right to both freedom and justice.

LEARNING TO SKATEBOARD IN A WARZONE (IF YOU'RE A GIRL)

CAROL DYSINGER; US; 2019; 39 MINS

In 2008, Australian skateboard enthusiast Oliver Percovich founded Skateistan, a grassroots education project in Kabul, Afghanistan. It soon developed into a school for girls aged between five and 17. By 2019, it was entirely run as a local education centre that also featured an indoor skateboard park. Carol Dysinger, who had been covering life in Afghanistan since the Soviet invasion, follows a new intake of girls over the course of a year, dividing time between the schoolroom and their skateboard lessons, the latter taught by two former students. The film highlights how both activities bolster the girls' confidence and how, in turn, their perception of the world widens. The Taliban's return to power in 2021 adds a bleak coda to the film's air of optimism. However, Dysinger and her colleagues were able to transport the school's teachers to safety before Afghanistan closed its borders.

INDEX

PICTURE CREDITS

ABOUT THE AUTHOR

Ian Haydn Smith is the author of *Selling the Movie*,
The Short Story of Photography, *FilmQuake*
and *Cult Writers*. He is a London-based
writer, editor and presenter.

ACKNOWLEDGEMENTS

Thanks to Pete Jorgensen for approaching me with
the original idea. And to Laura Bulbeck and Zara Anvari
for their patience and encouragement.
For a constant flow of documentary titles, thanks to
Helen de Witt, Nic Gibson, Mick McAloon and Mehelli Modi.
To Hannah, for ideas, good humour and putting up
with countless lists. And to Harry, my friend, who spent hours
discussing the merits of these and many other films with me.